INCLUSION IS FOR THE INCLUDED

A Collection of Short Stories
from A Special Needs Mom

by
La Taasha Byrd

The Grace of God, Inc.
Orlando   Los Angeles

Inclusion is for the Included: A Collection of Short Stories from a Special Needs Mom
Orlando, FL.

Published by The Grace of God, Inc.
Orlando, FL

Copyright © 2016 by The Grace of God, Inc.

Cover design by Tanika Ault of Legacy Designs c/o Graceful Lion Creations. Interior art by LeVaughn Stevenson. Photography by Angelo Davis.

All rights reserved, written permission must be secured from the publisher to use or reproduce any part of this book, except for brief quotation in critical reviews and articles.

No part of this publication shall be stored in a retrieval system of any sort nor transmitted, in any form by any means, electronic, mechanical, photocopying, recording or otherwise by anyone without prior permission of the publisher.

ISBN: 978-0-9800947-1-8

Published 2016. Printed in the United States of America.

If you would like to donate to Team Purple Pyramid for Step Up for Down Syndrome, visit our page at www.stepuporlando.kintera.org/purplepyramid or directly in our name to the Down Syndrome Association of Central Florida.

Inclusion is for the Included

*I'm dedicating this one to my favorite girl,
for where there was once four
there are now three*

Inclusion is for the Included

CONTENTS

	Dedication	iv
	Foreword	9
1	A Change in Season	13
2	A Most Beautiful Bouquet	23
3	Sign of the Times	35
4	Inclusion is for the Included	47
5	No Rest for the Weary	61
6	An Open Letter to an Expectant Special Needs Mom	69
7	ABCs…and IEPs	75
8	Train 'Em Up	85
9	Stop the R-Word	93
10	Pink and Yellow and Blue	109
11	Super Tuesday	115
	BONUS: Fifty Dimes and a Wrapper	135
	Acknowledgments	141
	About the Author	145

Inclusion is for the Included

Inclusion is for the Included

FOREWORD

I had not planned on telling my story to any particular person. Bits and pieces I had divulged here and there to a select few friends – and by select I DO mean carefully selected. I just had not felt comfortable talking with anyone. In those earliest days I felt as though no one would truly understand the magnitude of my feelings. I had a good friend once that revealed to me that she didn't know how to take me when I told her my inner feelings. She said I was just too deep for her to understand sometimes. That only made me revert further into the shell I had created for myself. I could tell my story to a complete stranger and feel better about it than talking to someone to whom I felt was 'close'. I wondered if I could ever find a closeness that wasn't fleeting, nor condescending, or with ulterior motives.

The circumstances surrounding the current state of affairs was a conundrum of sorts – the blessing that I was told had befallen me proved in my eyes a cursed, wretched nightmare that I could not wake from. Pinching would not work. Cold water would not work. And at times I felt that the prayers I so fervently petitioned would not work either. My faith had been shaken and I could not understand what had happened to the life that I once had. All that I knew was no more. Gone. Poof. In the blink of an eye. What was I to do? I had not a clue. What I did have was worries. A whole boatload of them. No...make that an ocean liner full. Try the Titanic, if you will. This last inference probably set the most relevant tone because my whole life had capsized and I didn't have a lifeboat nor could I swim. The water of my new life was frigid and bone-chilling. And there was not a star in sight in this vast darkness. So I retreated to the far recesses of my mind to a familiar place that I knew still existed, if only in the familiarity of my memories.

And I picked up a pencil.

This 'diary' of sorts started as a few random thoughts scribbled in no particular order or in any exact fashion. A legal pad here. A napkin there. Three or four lines saved to a hard drive. My mind overflowed with thoughts that screamed in their randomness. They echoed in the canyon that was my mind in a veritable cacophony of emotions and restless silent banter. I was a walking dichotomy, all the while appearing resilient while inside raged a war of deafening silence.

And I picked up a pen.

Words became my refuge. The power of the pen gave me strength that I remembered I had. As the words flowed from my mind to the page I felt a new sense of freedom: freedom from the world that I once knew and freedom to explore the new things that were to come. I was no longer bound to the spaces that my thoughts had confined themselves to, at my expense, but was able to reach a new level of awareness by sharing those instances that so vividly came to mind. The pen IS mightier than the sword. It has become my preferred weapon of choice to combat the ideologies which so vehemently seek to devour and hold captive the happy places in my life. I slay them with these words, for no longer will I be a prisoner to my own thoughts but rather a purveyor of the actions which will denigrate them.

I am no longer capsized. I stand upright. I am no longer shaken. I am stirred with a gift that could only be realized through adversity and made stronger with every stroke of the key. The broken melodies are now a brilliant symphony and I am the conductor.

Please enjoy this concerto, the first in a collection of

stories that bring the journey I have undertaken to light. May it fill your heart as it has healed mine. May you find a kindred bond in the mending of a shattered spirit and find the strength you might not have otherwise known. It is my wish that by sharing these experiences we may grow together. We are one and by breaking down the barriers that our minds build for us we learn to navigate uncharted waters and explore distant territories. We learn to help each other. We learn to live. We learn to thrive.

We do not sink.

We BECOME Titanic.

"If I could help somebody as I travel along then my living will not be in vain." ~Baptist Hymn

In love and wonder,

T

1

A CHANGE IN SEASON

'His eye is on the sparrow and I know He watches me.'
~Civilla Martin

For as long as I can remember, I've had an exceptional memory. At times photographic and at times triggered by sights or sounds, but nonetheless exceptional. When I was younger my mother would marvel at the information I could just seamlessly regurgitate at will. Case in point, I remembered once my grandmother tripped on a board that gave way on the back porch and I tried to break her fall and help her up. I knew that I was small, but mother informed me that I was only about three years old or so. How I could so vividly recall such things is beyond my understanding, but remarkable in any case. The same goes for conversations. Sometimes I can remember sentences verbatim, whole conversations emerging from the depths of my unconscious psyche. This would prove to be a gift at times, but other instances would manifest a deleterious rendering – a Trojan horse which invades my conscious under the guise of a gift and unleashes a cascade of heartache and despair.

Try as I might I could not file away nor make sense of the memories that were still agape from a gash that ripped apart everything that I understood. Exuberance had all but disappeared and despair had taken residence that winter. Four months had passed since that blustery January day. A fog had rolled in and engulfed everything that I once knew and my whole life had been changed in an instant. Since then each day had become a blur. They all ran into each other and the seams that held together day and night were ripped in the same manner as my heartstrings. I could not tell if I was coming or going. I lost track of moments, days, and weeks. If it had not been written down, it was not done. I could barely remember my name. I had not slept in what seemed like an eternity. My mind could not calm the sea of emotions that raged inside me. I tried to pray but I could not figure out exactly what to pray for. *Lord, help me* is all I could come up with. I looked in the mirror and did not recognize the image that stared back. I could not even remember who she was. All I *could* remember was that the doctors came into my room and sat down. Doctors never sit down.

On this day I was doing the sitting. The pseudo-solace of

my plush ivory lounger fed a three-fold purpose. In those days my wounds were still fresh, both mentally and physically. The side arm of the living room chair had become an optimum resting place and an excellent vantage point to view the goings on outside. I had come to favor the view of my tiny strip of a back yard. It was lined with oaks and just beyond the hedges was the main road. I would sit there, partly to relax, and partly to escape my own thoughts. I didn't have much of a choice though. That very same chair was my saving grace when I could not lie down after having surgery, but not by choice. I would have much rather escaped the confines of ninety-degree sleeping to embrace one supine comatose type of night. Those were not to be had, unfortunately. The thoughts kept getting in the way. Everything outside seemed to be an organized kind of chaos yet my mind was an organized kind of mess.

There was a family of squirrels that would forage under the oaks. They would start early in the morning and continue throughout the day. At some point they would retreat to the trees and in another instant chase each other back and forth. *'How wonderful it must be,'* I thought, *'to understand your purpose.'* These animals begin and end their days in full knowledge of what they would do and how they would go about doing it. They work together in concert unison, each going about their task with no reservation. *'The Lord takes care of them,'* I thought. '*The Lord takes care of them.*'

This particular day, however, felt vaguely familiar. It was a beautiful spring day. The traffic on the sidewalks of my neighborhood was steady with walkers. The sun outside my window was pleasant. The wind that whistled through the blinds sweetly kissed my cheek. Then just as suddenly I shuddered at the chill that enveloped my face. It was then that I realized that I had been crying. The tears fell and fell and the chill left in their wake scarred my cheeks like shattered glass. My body gave an involuntary shudder as they became more plenteous and the deluge was eminent. I could not have imagined that I would find myself in this weakened state. And I cried more. I could hear those words again, "...*we have some concerns about the baby*..." and I cried more. I dropped my head. And I cried even more.

My face was drenched and my heart was heavy. The day that was just so warm and inviting had faded away and I was sad beyond measure. How could my daughter have Down Syndrome? The memory of that day was as fresh as it ever was. I tried to recall things that would make me happy, but all I could focus on was the fact that I was completely clueless. Had I ruined her life by being her mother? I had no idea how to take care of her. Then I felt her move. I was so lost in my own head that I had completely forgotten that my daughter was lying in my arms. I looked down at the cute little pumpkin wrapped in a lavender blanket. I opened my eyes and met hers, a piercing stare with just a hint of a wrinkle between her eyes. She probed my glistening face and though she had no words to say her expression said everything. *'Why are you crying, Mommy?'* As I looked down at the life in my arms I realized that she had been watching me the entire time. I quickly wiped my face and attempted to regain my composure. I held her a bit tighter.

I could feel the warmth come over my face again. The squirrels were back at their job foraging and the goings on outside were still going on. I looked between the hedges and saw one car pass, then two. A mail truck had come to the side of the road and stopped. *'Well that's odd.'* I thought. There were no mailboxes on that side of the road, only the backs of the houses in my neighborhood. I moved to the edge of the chair to get a closer look. Then I saw a familiar face.

As the grayish-blue shorts-clad gentleman exited the truck I could see him in full view. It was my oldest and dearest friend. We had been friends since kindergarten and were now both in our thirties. I slowly stood and turned toward the sliding door. I set my little one in her bassinette and walked to the door. I slid the door back and walked into the sunlight.

"Heeey, my friend." he said with his arms opened wide.

"Well heeey yourself." I replied as I ducked between the hedges to meet his embrace. "Are you working hard or hardly working?"

"I'm working today." he said as he handed me my mail. "Where's my niece?" he asked.

"You want to see little mama? I'll go and get her." I said.

I tucked the mail under my arm, walked back through the hedges and past the sliding door to the bassinette beside the chair. I put the mail down, scooped up my daughter and the lavender blanket and headed back to the spot just beyond the hedges.

He leaned down and smiled close to her face. She looked back with a wide eyed stare.

"You see my little sack of potatoes?" I asked him. She was a little bundle of joy, not much more than seven pounds.

He replied with, "That's a SWEET potato!"

We laughed and he played with her as she wrapped her little hand around his finger. He talked to her in a voice that made me laugh and remember some of the crazy people we knew from high school days. In that instant I forgot that I had ever been upset. I felt a flood of good memories wash over my broken spirit and just as quickly as it was broken it was mended. I could feel my heart smile again. This is what happy felt like. This was a feeling that I remembered. And just as quickly as my friend appeared it was time for him to go. We waved as he went back to the mail truck and I maneuvered through the hedges with my sweet potato in tow, back through the sliding door, and into the house. I smiled to myself as I thought about those crazy high school days. I hoped that my daughter would grow to have those same memories that would make her laugh on a day that she did not quite feel like it. I sat with her in the comfy ivory chair.

In those days my home had become a sanctuary and a prison. My memories proved both to liberate and entomb me, but at that moment I chose the sanctuary. And so I sought it in a new realm. In order to produce a new effect, you had to do a new thing. In order to fill my heart, I first had to open it and let go of any and all things that were a hindrance to our happiness. Of all the things that I could remember, until then I could not ever recall knowing a love that could breathe new life, that was palpable, that could change hearts, that could erase bad memories. Then it happened. She looked into my eyes and smiled the biggest megawatt toothless grin I had ever seen. I knew then that we would be okay.

I knew then what I had to do. I opened my heart. I opened

my mind and gave myself permission to let it all go. I could not allow the memories that had once plagued me to remain a constant nemesis. I could not allow her diagnosis to disable the life I had planned we would have. No more negativity. No more 'yes'. Friends I had had for years, let go. Career I once loved, let go. Relationships, let go. The love of the velvety things, let go. In the grand scheme of things having her put my life in perspective in a way that only a few months before I could not fathom. All of a sudden the *latest* made no difference. I had not worked in months. Taking care of her held swift precedence over every waking moment. I had no time to think of the career that once sustained the lifestyle I had grown accustomed to. My days had been filled with doctors and specialists and tests and referrals and information and pamphlets and booklets. The friends that were once ever present were few and far in between. The shiny things had been replaced with baubles that had less luster. All that I once knew was no more and we were on our own. I was starting from zero with zero. Yet I was rich in spirit and had a fresh resolve to prove the naysayers wrong and blow the bell curve. She *would* be. I had allowed this newfound love to fill the spaces that once held the bad memories. I knew then that I was stronger than I thought. Her love had taught me that and I was all the better for it.

And what's more is that I realized that the prayer I prayed

when I did not know what to say was exactly the prayer that was answered. He heard me when I said, "*Lord, help me.*" He sent the animals to make me realize that all that I would ever need He would provide. He put them in a place where I could see them and set me in a mindset that made me fully aware. He sends us comforters when we are weary to lend a kind word or simply remove our thoughts from dwelling on a sad situation. He said that He would never leave nor forsake us. As I thought about the new life we would forge together I could hear a quiet rustling just beyond the sliding door. The squirrels had come back. I thought to myself again, '*The Lord takes care of them*' and surely He would take care of us.

Inclusion is for the Included

2

A MOST BEAUTIFUL BOUQUET

'Can't piss in my face and call it rain.'
~Mattie Henry

This journey throughout motherhood takes many twists and turns. There are many times when we have a clear path but many others which the opposite prevails. As a matter of fact, most days are difficult. Let me rephrase that: every day is difficult. The decisions you have to make have no clear right or wrong, but rather ambient shades of grey that wax and wane as the days progress. Add a child with a disability of any sort and the game changes entirely. Though our children are far more alike other children than different, parenting takes on a whole new persona. Being a special needs mom is an entity unto itself, for those who do not live this life firsthand cannot fully grasp the intrinsic realm of medical, therapeutic, emotional, and mental nuances that many do not ever have to encounter. Until I became a mother I had not been exposed to the subtle, and not so subtle, ways that your feelings can be viewed. Up until then it was always the *'well, you don't understand because you don't have kids'* type of insult that I often endured. I begged to differ. Empathy is like common sense. You either have it or you do not. I have come to trust my gut feelings, those emotional pangs that tug, and at times rip, my heartstrings. My adrenaline is stored in fight mode and Mama Bear is never far away. I do not like always being in beast mode, but you have to do what you have to do. Mess with my baby and 'you gone learn today.'

I had only been a mother for about three days and I was just getting used to being called 'Mom' much less understanding all the medical terminology that I was being forced to learn so quickly. I was a Biology/Pre-Medicine major in college and medical terminology was one of the courses I aced. Who knew that later on I would have to recall all of those terms during a time that was so emotional? I could easily decipher the diagnoses and knew what they would say before they would try to explain. In that respect, understanding was easy. What was difficult was the comprehending because for the life of me I just KNEW they were lying. This was all a dream and I was going to wake up pretty soon. I just had to trust my instincts and pray to God for strength.

And clarity.

And more strength.

And more clarity.

On that third day I had a feeling that something was not quite right with my daughter, but every time that I would voice a concern the medical staff would dismiss my thoughts as me being paranoid and overly cautious. '*Is this your first child?*' they would ask. 'What #*&@ difference does that make?' I kept thinking to myself. I was waaaaaay over the condescending tone of the medical staff at this point. Whether or not I had a child before did not make my concern any less valid, yet each time a new technician would come in to take my vitals or the nurses changed shifts, I had another dismissal to add to the pile. We were discharged on the fourth day and though I never did get a straight answer as to why I felt the way that I did, I wrapped my baby in a pretty lavender blanket and we went home.

Needless to say that first night home was the most frightening night of my life. I was new to absolutely everything and though my mother and grandmother were there to help me, there had not been a baby in the house in thirty-five years. So much had changed since they were in charge of an infant. Yet with the power of three and a God that hears and answers prayers we made it.

The next night DD (my dear daughter) had stopped nursing well. I thought maybe I wasn't doing it right. I really didn't know what to think. I kept a log of every feeding and diaper change for the next day's appointment. *'Surely I'm being paranoid,'* I thought. But was I really?!?

Sleep deprived as I was that nagging feeling never did leave and when it was time for us to take my daughter back to the doctor for her first check-up I asked the same questions of them. I was fortunate to have an EXCELLENT RNP (registered nurse practitioner) helping me with lactation that actually took the time to listen. I told her that I was having a hard time getting my daughter to nurse and she immediately started asking questions. She listened intently as I told her about the night we had. At one point she left the room for a few minutes and came back with a doctor that I had not seen before.

Then it started.

Before I knew it New Doctor left and a tech came in with a cart trailing behind. She took my daughter's vitals again and as she began to document the information, RNP and New Doctor were back with a tiny bassinette and a stack of papers.

"Mom," they said, "we would like for you to sign these consent papers for us to perform a few tests on your daughter...spinal tap...blood and urine sample...sign, initial and date..."

I looked at my own mom. She had a bewildered look on her face. I was wondering why she was not answering them. Then it struck me: I am MOM. They are talking to *me*. I am MOM. I have to sign these papers. I have to make the decisions. I am MOM.

Lord, help me.

I took a deep breath to clear my head. I turned back toward the RNP and New Doctor as they explained the types of tests they wanted to run. I tried to listen intently but my mind was racing like Dale Sr. in the #3 car and I just could not calm myself enough to make a sane decision. RNP noticed that I was having a hard time and told me that they would leave the papers for us to review but would only take my daughter with them after we gave consent. I did then and started to sign the packet. I kissed my baby girl and placed her in the bassinette. I felt as helpless as a torn piece of paper. A light gust of wind would have blown me right over.

New Doctor came back after some time and told me that they were going to admit my daughter to the hospital and they were sending the ambulance for her. I sent Mom out to check on my grandmother while I went to see my little one. She was under a yellow light warming up in a sheet that looked like aluminum foil. The EMTs came with a stretcher that would later hold my tiny six-pound baby and a whole lot of other machines and wires that were larger than she was. They helped me into the front of the ambulance. I could not sit in the back because I had just had a C-section and could not lift my leg onto the bumper and pull myself up nor could I walk faster than a whopping half mile per hour. We rode a terrifying half mile to the emergency room and I zombie shuffled through the hospital doors holding on to the stretcher that carried my daughter, past the intake station, to the elevators, and up to the floor where we would stay for the next week while my little one got better.

We were alone. Just me and her. I look back on that time and think about how those early moments were a foreshadow of things to come. I didn't know it then but I was fighting for her. I had to pull myself together to make the tough decisions at five days just as I would later at five years. Throughout all the tears and the breakdowns, I made it. *We* made it. We're *still* making it. And I'm *still* fighting.

Nine days and a roller coaster of emotions later we left the hospital. The discharge papers stated that DD had a UTI and was septic. I knew then that my intuition was not leading me wrong. I had it, that Mother's Wit. I had heard about it and now I knew for myself that it was not a myth. From then on I wouldn't let ANYONE tell me that I was wrong. I had this. I'm a MOM.

Some time later I was watching the television show 'Dr. G: Medical Examiner' and saw an episode that seemed a bit too close to home. It was about a young girl with a week old baby girl who died at home. The autopsy revealed that the infant had contracted an infection which was why she had stopped eating and reacting normally before dying in her sleep. I broke down and wailed until my eyes and throat burned. If I had not insisted on someone listening to me that could have very well been me. This particular television show was shot in the county I lived in. I thanked God for Mother's Wit. I had it. Thank God. I had it.

A few months passed and I celebrated my first Mother's Day and though I was happy to be a celebrant I was still riding the roller coaster. DD was still rather sickly and I was learning to navigate the ups and downs of my own emotional state while understanding what I needed to take care of her. I would often retreat to an online message board where I found a great group of moms who shared similar stories and were a great source of comfort. Sometimes they were my only source of comfort. I felt so alone most times. My daughter was eight months old, I had not gone back to work, and I was the only one of my friends who had a child with special needs. While they had all gone back to their lives before children, I was learning to begin a new life. So I was happy to find a note someone left for me in my inbox one day. It made me feel so much better when I saw that someone that I didn't even know cared enough to let me know that they were thinking of me. It read:

I don't do this often...but I wanted to send you a note because I am a member...and I was touched by your original post when you first had your baby girl and were coping with her diagnosis. Every once in a while I look for your posts to see how you are and have been amazed by how much you've learned about therapies and are moving forward and the incredible love and strength you show your little one. I have a 7 month old son, he doesn't have DS, but there are certain mamas' posts that have inspired me or who give great info and I decided to let them know.

Anyway, I felt like a lurker and so I just thought I'd let you know. Congrats on your beautiful baby girl.

That was six years ago. Since then we've had many more hospital stays. The doctors have become friends. We see an army of specialists, therapists, advocates, and the like. It's always Mother's Day in some capacity when you have a child with special needs. I'm her strongest advocate. I'm Mama Bear. I don't mind bearing my claws. Or my teeth. When she needs me I go into full beast mode. The Mother's Wit takes over and I don't miss a beat because I am MOM. I make the tough decisions.

One year DD got sick at the dinner table while we were out to eat. The poor waitress kept trying to offer me another meal to take home but I didn't want it. I just wanted to take her home and get her well. I've had many comped meals since then as well. Somehow Mother's Day has taken on a new form for me. I celebrate, but in my own way. One year I woke to my favorite episode of 'Monk' (Mr. Monk and the Panic Room) playing to a quiet house. That was a great present. No one was awake and I was in heaven. It's funny how such little things bring you joy when you have had such adversity. I laughed like it was the first time that I had ever seen it. That was a great day.

Inclusion is for the Included

Yesterday I was tending my garden and I heard little feet behind me. As I pulled the weeds from the vegetable bed she decided to pull some things as well. Every so often I would peek over to see what she was doing. She would lean down, then get up, chase a lizard or two on the fence, and pick up a small rock to throw. As I turned to put the newly picked weeds in a bag she came to me with something in her had. My first instinct, that Mother's Wit, was to tell her to put those weeds down, but I didn't. She held a bouquet of tiny wildflowers in her hand. She said, "Here Mommy." My heart melted. That was the most beautiful bouquet I have ever gotten. There is not a florist in the world that could make one better.

"Thank you, baby." I said. I guess she heard me. She was already off chasing another lizard. This year I had another quiet Mother's Day. My daughter took a nap. I took a nap. It was a GREAT day. I thought about a post that I had written in that online message board from my second Mother's Day that read:

Mother's Day 2011:

With all of the trials and emotional sacrifices we as a community have had to endured, and mainly due to no particular fault of our own, I wanted to say just how much I have appreciated being a part of such a great group of people.

Though we do not all know each other personally the common thread that binds us is one which is woven into a wonderful quilt that warms my heart on the coldest days ever.

Perhaps this is a birthday of sorts - a day set aside to celebrate the emergence of a kindred appreciation that only a Mother could understand.

So thank you for your concerns and well wishes, rants and raves, brags and tears, for you all are Super Moms and I salute you.

Have a wonderful Mother's Day. Now pass the banana pancakes....

Have a wonderful everyday Mother's Day good people. Use your wit. I know I will. You can't piss in my face and call it rain. (I got that from my mama)

3

SIGN OF THE TIMES

*"Keep puttin' one foot in front the other.
You'll get there after 'while".* ~Mattie Henry

Since becoming a mom, and a special needs mom at that, I have become accustomed to the incessant hustle and bustle of the day. What many will do all day can be accomplished in an hour or two in our household. It is not unforeseeable that by 7 am on any given morning I have started breakfast, washed last night's dishes, fixed juice, repaired furniture, found some mystery item, deciphered the daughter code, cleaned the juice that I just fixed, rinsed, reloaded, and repeated it all in about thirty minutes. I am tugged and pulled and rubbed and patted, all in attempts to get my attention, because as of yet my DD cannot speak clearly. I feel a tug at my leg and as I look down I see a chubby fourteen-month-old little person looking up at me with an intent gaze, waving her hands and motioning. To anyone else it would seem as though she was just gesturing, but she is talking to me. She moves a partially closed hand in a C-shape back and forth in front of her mouth. She wants a drink. I opened the refrigerator door. '*Let's try this juice thing one more time*' I thought to myself. I fixed another juice cup and handed it to her. She reached for it and put the straw in her mouth.

I took it from her.

"What do you say?" I said as I handed the cup back to her.

She reached her little hands out again and this time, before she put the straw in her mouth, she gestured a hand away from her mouth. It looked like she blew me a kiss, but this was her saying 'thank you.'

"You're welcome." I said with a smile. Manners must be taught and even though my daughter could not yet talk I refused to raise an impolite, self-absorbed, I want, gimme gimme child. Her being non-verbal made absolutely no difference. There were plenty of ways to be polite and I had no problem in being the enforcer. She smiled back and then she was off to meet the Wizard, the Wonderful Wizard of Oz.

It is a tireless, thankless job that mere mortals will never see. It must be lived to be fully appreciated. In the years that have passed I have come to know many others like me. It is a society of superheroes who don invisible capes and spring into action to care for the loved ones in their charge. I was fortunate that we needed mostly therapy and our hospital stays were relatively brief and conclusive. Special needs parenting comes in many shapes and sizes. Learning to adapt to each challenge as it comes is par for the course. So when I thought about learning to sign I dug through my old college textbooks and found the manual I used for an elective class in sign language. I never knew why I kept that book. I did not know anyone who was deaf and had only used the signs I learned once before with a friend that I met who was deaf but who read lips very well. She barely signed herself. Yet as fate would have it, here I was with a child that needed to learn and I was much obliged to teach her.

I started to teach DD to sign when she was about seven months old. I would sit her in her high chair and sign every item I would put in front of her: milk, juice, fruit, crackers, cookies, etc. Snacks were a great motivator and though she wasn't eating many solids I added to the sign vocabulary as she started to eat more. She learned to ask for 'more', and to sign 'please' and 'thank you'. The high chair was her first school desk and this way I had her full attention. The food gave way to flash cards with common words and pictures of household objects. I taught her to 'sign and say' each item and she responded very well. By the time she was two years old she had a signing vocabulary well over one hundred words. Her occupational therapist would often prompt her to say 'I want' but could never get a response. I had to let her know that 'I want' is a command, and she has to ask politely for what she would like to have. I told her OT (occupational therapist) to try 'have please' and just like that DD was following her instructions. I was fortunate in having a wonderful OT that listened to me and valued my input as a parent. This is not always the case. I would find this out as our journey continued, much to my dismay.

One of the first memories I had of DD signing outside our home was at a therapy session with her OT. DD was about ten months old in a session working on her pincer grasp and using cereal to pick up. There were cheerios on the table where she was seated and apparently DD had enough of them because she signed 'all done' and cleared all those cheerios in one fell swoop. Then she moved her hands in the air to do it again. 'All done' looks like the gesture for 'safe' in baseball when a player slides in to home base. Both the OT and I laughed at the flying cheerios but were proud just the same that she was learning to communicate. I knew then that I had made a solid choice in teaching her to sign. She could use her hands to say what she could not with words.

A few months later there was a statewide convention for Down Syndrome and I attended the pre-conference sessions with DD in tow. There was a table with several food platters set up for the opening reception and as I made a plate for myself I could see her squirming in my periphery. She looked up at me from the stroller and signed 'crackers'. This sign looks like a closed fist on one hand tapping on a bent elbow of the opposite arm. Another DS mom was standing next to me and saw her. She had a daughter who was hard-of-hearing and knew instantly that DD was asking for crackers. I was beaming like a peacock by then. I put several crackers on her stroller tray. She smiled and signed 'thank you.' She knew full well that if she didn't those crackers were getting picked up with the quickness. I felt so great that night, partly because DD was getting used to communicating and partly because someone else understood her. At the opening session I only heard about half of what the opening speaker said. I was still on a cloud because my DD had signed 'crackers'.

From then on it was full steam ahead. DD was only about thirteen months old and I started learning every sign I could so that I could teach her. I got discouraged at the videos I would find because they would only show signs singularly and not in phrasing. And furthermore, we had exhausted all the 'baby signs' that I could find in books. There were many more signs than milk, more, and mommy. I scoured the internet and finally came upon a website that had an extensive dictionary plus videos for phrasing. I found a few local classes that taught signing free of charge. I tried to absorb as much information as I could about signing in general, ASL, and deaf culture so that I could teach my daughter. What I knew she would know. I was determined. By any means necessary. I signed everywhere so that she would learn new words.

I was constantly asked if she was deaf, to which I would simply reply, "No". Then the barrage of questions would ensue. 'Why are you signing with her if she can hear?' and 'When is she going to start talking?' were a few of the most frequent questions I heard. Having a child with special needs puts a target on your back. People seem to always have something to say, a method for you to try, or some information that surely you have never thought of. While many are basically nice it never ceases to amaze me how insensitive some people can be. Some people have a genuine concern while others were just down-right nosey and disingenuous. Rude often comes to mind. I try to use each experience as an opportunity to educate but it wears you down. Through the years I have learned to take the comments in stride and throw massive shade when needed. I can set a naysayer in their place at fifty paces. I do NOT play about my baby. Not even with the good church folk.

After a Sunday morning church service, a member approached me. She was a staunch pro laureate for education and didn't mind letting it be known. Often she would lead the charge for tutoring and scholarship drives for members in their quest for higher learning.

"Why do you sign to this baby?" She asked. "She's going to talk."

Apparently she had noticed me during the service. I sign the words JESUS and PRAISE and HEAVEN as I hear them being said. DD signs them in agreement. She claps her hands and raises them to the sky. She knows that in this venue she is free. Where the spirit of God is, there is liberty...even for a fifteen-month-old.

"Why do you ask?" I replied.

I tried not to answer in a defensive tone, but I had to call on the Father, Son, and the Holy Ghost to not go completely off. First off, I had simply not gotten used to the unsolicited advice that I would get from EVERYWHERE concerning DD. I'm a brand new mom. I get it. She has Down Syndrome. I get that, too. But would people scrutinize everything that a typically developing child did...even from people they didn't know that well? Or did being in church give them the right to say whatever was on their mind?

"This baby is going to talk. You just have to keep saying the words. See...ball, ball, ball, ball....ball..." she said. She gestured a pointed finger toward her mouth as DD looked on bewildered.

DD raised her hands and made a circular motion with them, tapping her fingers together. BALL. She just signed BALL.

Higher education did not even notice. She just kept saying BALL. I wanted to scream. She just signed BALL and she did not know it. Nor did I feel at that point she even cared.

I chimed in, "Well, she can't talk *NOW*...and signing helps her to communicate *NOW*. I know she will speak, but since she needs to communicate *NOW* I'll keep signing to her. She just signed what you said, too. *BALL*."

"Well, you just keep working with her," she said, "and she'll talk. You just watch." Higher education walked away and began to talk to another member. They were soon engaged in a lively banter and the previous conversation had faded to black.

I dropped my head and shook it in disbelief. "Jesus..." I said. I looked over at DD in my arms. She signed JESUS. In that instant all the negativity that I felt melted away and a wry little smile crossed my pursed lips. *She gets it*, I thought. We understand each other.

That was five years ago. During those early years I had a hard time adjusting. My feelings were always on my shoulder, real close to the surface. I found solace in an online community of moms who were going through similar situations. I would read every day and often respond in kind. There was one post in particular that caught my attention. It was about a mom whose husband didn't like signing and was discouraging the ST (speech therapist) to stop because he thought it was a crutch, whereas she felt it was a support structure. I sat at my computer and wrote this:

I always thought that I would teach my baby signs and when my daughter was born, signing seemed natural because she cannot yet speak. I have fought therapists, educators, and naysayers who think that her signing will discourage her speaking. What I generally tell them is that she learns differently and the signing is something that she learns WELL. So she can communicate her thoughts and we understand each other.

DD learns well through movement. She tries to speak her signs and is learning phrases. I don't care if her therapists advise against ASL because it does not follow standard English formatting, but I see it as a second language and a skill that will help her in her journey toward spoken language. And being bilingual is a plus even if the second language is not actually heard.

She will be expected 'not to' and 'discouraged from' things more or less for the rest of her life and I WILL NOT START IT IN MY HOME. If it works for her, then it works for me.

And in that order.

I checked my inbox on the community page a little later and found several responses, too numerous to list here, but the general consensus was that many agreed with me. One, however, stood out from the rest. It read:

I just read your reply on the [board] about when to stop using sign language. You wrote "She will be expected 'not to' and 'discouraged from' things more or less for the rest of her life and I WILL NOT START IT IN MY HOME. If it works for her, then it works for me. And in that order." And when I read that, I teared up a little bit, because it was so beautifully written.

I have since continued to teach DD to sign and now she knows more than her teachers, therapists, doctors and basically anyone she comes in contact with in the hearing realm. She signs her Easter speech and can negotiate like none other for any afternoon snack. I still get asked if she is deaf a lot, but I don't feel so guarded now. I just say, "No." and leave it at that. Many then ask, "How do I say _____". These are great advocacy and teachable moments. I often instruct DD to show them the sign. These moments make me feel proud. And happy. And prouder. And happier.

DD started school at the age of three in a preschool class filled with children with varying exceptionalities. The teacher that she had was so supportive. One Valentine's Day DD came home with a backpack full of trinkets and candy and cards and papers. I opened it and found this:

Inclusion is for the Included

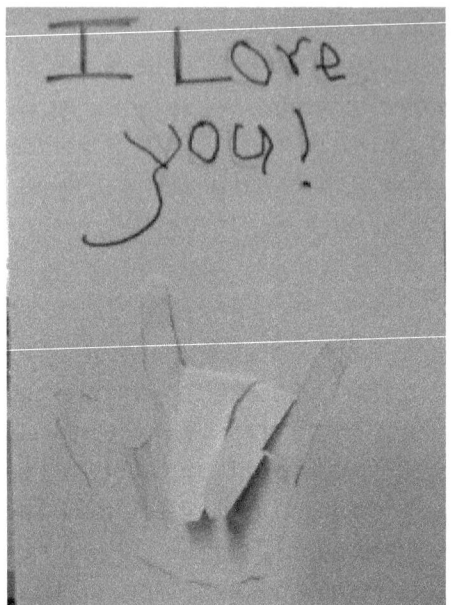

Her teacher had helped her to make a card with the sign for 'I Love You' on the front in a cut-out of her hand. I felt a tear roll down my cheek. She has a teacher that *gets it*. She understands us.

And in that order.

4

INCLUSION IS FOR THE INCLUDED

*'You never know a person 'til you have
dealins' with 'em.'* ~Mattie Henry

It's Monday night at 8 pm. There is a three-compartment plate resting on a mini table with remnants of what was once a mini meal of chicken fingers and vegetables. The television is set to ABC. There is a slight pause from the last commercial and then I hear a familiar tune.

The beloved chicken fingers have been abandoned and DD has commenced to twirling. 'Dancing With the Stars' is on and everything is right with the world. *This must be a pretty special show*, I think to myself, *to make her put those chicken fingers down.* The ballroom is awash in glitz and glamor and the costumes are equally as ritzy. DD has picked out her favorite dress and handed it to me. *Dress...dress...*she signs with those cute little hands, all the while the twirling still continues. I look at her kindly, sign, and say, "No, no..." because I know this is a set up. Once the clothes come off, the clothes will stay off. Not today, Chica.

An hour has passed. The dancers have danced. DD has remembered the chicken fingers and is captively watching as the couples finish and stand to receive their scores. "THREE!!!!" she exclaims as the first judge lifts her paddle. "THREE!!!!" she exclaims as the second judge lifts his paddle. "THREEEEEE!!!!" she exclaims as the third judge lifts his paddle. She claps wildly with excitement and runs to me and lifts her hands. We twirl in our own rendering of a Viennese Waltz. I put her down and she signs, *Mommy...dance...mommy...please*. I looked at my two-year-old with those chubby thick legs, ever twirling, and signed and said, 'Okay'.

I found a dance class for little ones and I asked the coordinator if she gave private lessons as well. After finding out the logistics I told her that DD receives a community scholarship for activities she might participate in alongside her peers. She assured me that once the classes started she would let me know. The director was a girl that I knew from church who was a dancer and had newly opened a small dance studio not far from the main sanctuary. I had seen the work that she had done with the little girls as they danced on Youth Sunday and was eager to have my little one join the troop. They all seemed so happy in their little outfits, jumping and dancing and rejoicing in the Lord. It all seemed so innocent. What better way to help my little one with her physical therapy in an atmosphere of love and compassion all the while teaching her the valued effort that is teamwork and confidence.

That was three years ago.

Yes. I did say THREE.

I would sit in the congregation during Sunday service and watch little girls dance and spin to the music and DD would try her hardest to get out of the pew. Again I would ask when the new classes would start. As yet I have never gotten a confirmation. So it was much to my surprise when I received a text from the coordinator asking a favor. She was having a recital and needed a few outfits made. I looked at the phone in my hand in puzzled bewilderment. I had been asking for lessons for my baby for three whole years and now she is asking me for a favor for yet another performance that DD won't participate in. I had to appeal to ALL of my Christian sensibilities not to go off because the petty train leaves my house E'ER DAY at unspecified times. As a matter of fact, I felt the train rolling in as I stood there. Yet I took a quick breath and thought carefully how to respond.

I hit the reply button and the text screen popped up. I looked at it intently. Then I decided against writing. I hit the phone icon and waited on the ring. One ring. Two rings. Three rings. Voicemail. "Oh well," I thought to myself. I left a message stating that I would call back later.

When I did get a chance to speak to her I told her that I would help with her project. I told her the pricing per item and the options available in terms of fabric and upgrades. She stated that she didn't have much money but perhaps we could come to make some type of arrangement to which I knew EXACTLY what I would ask for. I told her that if she paid for the fabric I would give her the wholesale price and to give my baby private lessons to offset the balance in monetary payment. I felt this was more than fair. My grandmother used to say 'an even swap ain't a swindle.' This way DD could finally dance with the little ones. Finally. Three years later. Three whole years later.

I got to work making the order for extra fabric and all the notions I would need to get the project started. In the midst of the week it took to gather all that I needed I was handed another blow to our routine: DD's therapies were

Inclusion is for the Included

about to change and there was suddenly no wiggle room available for her to have dance lessons. I felt awful that again these elusive lessons had yet again escaped our grasp. I continued with the project, however, and delivered on time. I had DD with me that night of the delivery but I didn't let her come into the studio. I just didn't want her to see the other little ones dancing and she not be able to. So I took her to a friend of mine while I went to work. The parents were ecstatic and the little ones were equally happy as they fitted their outfits. They looked like little angels. I was proud of the work that I had done. And then the bubble burst when a few of the parents approached me and said,

"Why don't you let DD dance?"

The wind just left my sails. AGAIN. I could feel the petty rolling up from my feet. Yet I would never disrespect another fellow business owner in their own establishment no matter the situation. I'm much better than that. Even though I wanted to scream that I had been trying to get DD lessons for YEARS and unload all my special needs mom frustrations on anyone who would listen I would never air dirty laundry for all to see. No, not this girl. Not this day. Not ANY day. I'm much better than that. I really wanted to though. REALLY. Right then I could feel the petty in my bones.

I looked at them with a smile and said, "Maybe later. We have a full plate right now," and commenced to sizing again.

I finished sizing and gathered the outfits to give to the coordinator, who was frantic with parents and little dancers and music and whatnot. I pulled her to the side and told her that I would contact her about our arrangement, as a portion of the terms would need to change. She said, 'okay' and went back to frantic some more. I left to gather my little one. What should have been an easy project had left me feeling some kind of way. The only caveat was that DD didn't have a clue. She was as happy as she could be riding shotgun and watching her favorite DVD as we rode home.

The performance was five days later. Two more days had passed and I still hadn't heard from the coordinator. I picked up the phone and sent this text:

Good morning. I haven't heard from you. I will send you a letter for all that I wanted to speak to you about. It will also contain an invoice for services. DD's therapies are now up to five/week so additional private lessons are not an option at this time. This compensation will go toward her college fund, as do a portion of all my sales...If you have photos please forward them so I can include them on my site and

FB page and give your studio some publicity. Talk to you later. Be blessed.

Sometime the next day I received this note:

GM...I have been stupid busy...studio, work...and personal life focused. Yesterday was the first day our sweet little (ones) were able to put on (the outfits) and dance in them. Needless to say they are a big hit. The kids love them. The parents love them. I love them. I will be definitely taking pictures of them. I was hoping you were coming to the Program today. I would love to introduce you to the parents. (Bring your business cards just in case). Now for our agreement. I don't have money but I will try and get some of the parents to donate for your services. However, I thought the idea of private lessons as our trade out was going to be a great start to get your baby the dance lessons you want her to have. I also think this will help me to learn how to teach a special needs child. I hope we can still stick to our agreement. This could be such a blessing for us both. There is a divine reason why we are finally working together. Let's let God do HIS thing. I know you feel I have not said much about you, your child and your awesome work. But please know my heart. I do care and so appreciate all that you have done for the ministry. I know your dream is to see your baby dance. Let's do it then. Let's try it first in a few private lessons setting. I can explain to you in person why I know this is best. Let me know when you want to talk. I thank God for you. Have a wonderful Holiday season and I hope to talk to you soon...

After I read this I knew that my work was not going to be repaid. There was just no room in this scheduling to have anything extra. Absolutely none. What many people do not understand about children with special needs is that they get over-stimulated VERY quickly. The constant pull on every angle is incessant and as a parent I must discern how much is too much. This was going to be too much. So I called the coordinator and told her how I felt about the whole situation. Then I put pen to paper and hand-delivered the note along with an invoice for service for roughly thirty-percent of the wholesale price. Thirty percent of the sixty-percent off wholesale price. I wasn't even getting paid a quarter of what I usually charge because I wanted to be fair, but I also didn't think that it was fair for us to not receive any compensation at all. I was barely working in those days. I depended on every order to get us through the rough times. I had only the thought that since I had done something for someone, good would come back to me no matter the circumstances. My blessing would come and it would benefit both me and DD.

Two weeks later there was still no definite response.

Okay. I'm done.

That was a year and a half ago. I had long since stopped believing that DD would somehow miraculously either get lessons or I would be paid somehow. I just let it go. This was not a fight that I was willing to pursue. Kindergarten was coming up and that required everything that I had left in me. Dancing was no longer high on the priority list. I needed to focus on getting her ready for full-time school in a general education kindergarten class. I needed to mentally prepare for the push-back that would inevitably ensue. I needed to put all my energy into what was sure and would not offer any sleepless nights.

Non-inclusion by silence is confirmation enough. Often special needs families are not responded to in a manner timely enough to be included in any given activity. Sadly, we have come accustomed to this type of behavior. Whether intentional or not, many see a child with an exceptionality as a challenge. Rightfully so, for the obstacles that are set before us are clear and present. They are ever changing, nonconforming, and all consuming. That does not mean, however, that they cannot be overcome. A hurdle placed before you is just that: a hurdle. It is not meant to remain a mainstay on the track. You must jump over them. They don't move for *you*. You must move over *them*. In some cases, you just have to lift your leg and kick them right over and off the track. Then drag them under the stands.

In changing the current of non-inclusion I am a front and present type of mom. I do not see DD and her differing abilities as a hindrance. Where there is an opportunity, there we are. At each IEP (Individualized Education Plan) meeting I have gone in... ALONE. I bring every accolade in my arsenal and champion the good that she CAN do. I document EVERYTHING. I read and familiarize myself with the law and what is entitled so that she may receive an education in the least restrictive manner possible. If needed, I flow against the current because I am her advocate. I know that the school must protect their interests. I must protect mine as well. Fiercely. My grandmother used to say that only a mighty poor frog wouldn't praise his own pond. Well...we have OCEAN praise over here.

I originally wrote about this incident on my blog, Countdown To K. I posted it to my FB (Facebook) page as well as to a parent's group, Inclusion for Children with Down Syndrome. To my surprise, I was reprimanded for posting what I thought was allowed content in the group. Furthermore, the administrators removed me from the group, citing that I was trying to promote my blog. Wow. I can't adequately express how I felt reading this:

Hi everyone..

We want to thank everyone that helps to keep this group running smooth.. hard to do with such a large group. It should be pretty clear by now that we would like for the group to stay on topic.. this is exactly why the group is helpful to so many and remains as successful as it is.

That said.. the spam, self-promotion and off topic posting is getting out of hand. The admins do not have the time to sit around all day putting out unnecessary fires. Moving forward, we will be deleting and removing members from the group if we notice they are not playing by the rules, without notice. The rules and intentions of the group are very clear and really easy to understand.

I love how helpful this group is to so many, myself included.. and this is the reason that we have the rules we have. It isn't that we don't appreciate some of the off topic posts.. it is just that we want this group to remain strictly about education related topics. Thank you!!

'Wow' is all I could muster. After resubmitting a request to join and being re-allowed into the group, I wrote a response saying that I posted the article because I had more to say than could be written in a simple post and that I felt very 'un-included' by the very group that self-proclaims inclusion for children. The post may have helped someone in the same situation. And guess what? The administrators removed my post. So you see, inclusion IS for the included and even a fellow special needs parent can be un-invited to the show. There is a sanctimonious hierarchy in even the most trivial of groups. Cliques are ever rampant. There is always a faction that will express the need to govern and, in essence, exclude. I don't post there anymore. The group is just too horribly depressing, not to mention all the problems that other parents have with inclusionary tactics waged by school systems across the country. I prefer to direct my energy to more positive avenues. Many things have changed since that first IEP and these non-inclusionary incidents. DD has progressed both educationally and socially in so many ways. She can sign VERY well, often knowing more signs than the therapists, doctors, and teachers. This year she signed, and said, her Easter speech. She ice skates in a program for children with special needs and their siblings. Last year she was awarded 'Most Improved Skater' as she no longer needed her walker on the ice. She is learning to ride horseback. Who knows.... we may have a jumper in our midst. And she sings in the children's choir at church just like I did when I was her age. I raise her the way that I was raised. I teach her to love people and to do what is right even if you feel that you have been slighted. Keep your head up and keep moving forward.

All of this is possible with people placed around you with the right attitude about inclusion. Children must be taught that they are different. They play and interact with other children innocently. Remember when we were told as children to go and make friends? If you didn't immerse yourself into the mix, you had to play alone. Inclusion works the same way. It only works with active participants. It must be practiced wholeheartedly. It must be joyful and vibrant, not reserved and silent. Barriers are there but through the tenacity of this super-charged mom and the stick-to-it-tiveness of my can-do DD we will take on those barriers and remove them one hurdle at a time.

DD may still not dance formally, but we can Viennese Waltz in our all-inclusive private dance floor living room. I'll read to her about the injustices we encountered early in our journey and later she will read them for herself. I will advocate for her until my last breath so her card will be full of suitors. And come August we are going to dance right into that first grade classroom.

Now twirl on that.

Twice.

Inclusion is for the Included

5

NO REST FOR THE WEARY

"I ain't NEVER seen a baby don't sleep..."
~Mattie Henry

I'm awakened from a not-so-deep sleep by a loud and startling noise. My DD had turned over and, in all her flailing glory, hit the wall that her bed rests against. Now I'm wide awake. Again. The glaring glow of my clock/radio emits a piercing stare that I have grown accustomed to. 1:24 am. I close my eyes for a minute and attempt to roll over. *Maybe she'll fall back asleep*, I think. Then I hear it again. If I didn't know any better, I would think that a wrecking ball had just demolished a portion of my house and my poor baby is hidden somewhere in the rubble.

I had walked this zombie mile from my room to hers twice already this night. She finally fell asleep after MUCH fanfare around 10:30 pm. She had sprawled across my body in some unfortunate pretzel shape that didn't make moving her conducive to keeping my wretched back intact. I knew that I needed to pick up this sack of flour, take her to the room, and tuck her in. I was just leery of trying to get up too fast and falling back down onto the couch or trying to get up before she was in a deep enough sleep and risk her waking up again. I chose the former because my arms were starting to lose sensation and I was dozing myself. *Okay...brace yourself*, I thought. She was real cute...and REAL HEAVY. Don't let that cuteness fool you because picking her up while she was in a deep sleep was like doing a clean and jerk in weightlifting competition. I started rocking back and forth to get some momentum. One, two, three and I finally made it to my feet. I braced the backs of my legs against the couch and just stood there trying to get myself together. *About twenty-five steps and I'm there. Just one foot in front of the other and I'm there. Just one foot and then the other.* My body hadn't quite caught up with my thought process because my right leg had fallen asleep. I could feel the pins doing an elaborate dance with every nerve ending in my leg, plus I was holding Heavy Heavy. Now I'm REALLY doing the zombie shuffle with Ms. Ma'am in my arms. Twenty-two more steps to go. Let's do this.

Lawd hammercy. I can't hardly make it.

I thought that I might just stop and lay down in the middle of the floor, but then I'd have to get up again. I took a deep breath and held Big Block a little tighter. My arms were burning but I knew that waking her up was NOT an option. I kept shuffling until I made it to her room. I walked through the doorway and past the play kitchen and felt all the energy that I had mustered up previously wash from my body: the bed hadn't been turned down. Why would it, I thought. She didn't take a nap today. She had been going full throttle ALL DAY and so the bed hadn't been touched since I made it this morning. I thought about putting her in the bed on top of the comforter but if she had an accident I'd have to wash the comforter, the sheet, the fitted sheet, AND the chuck that was under her IF I was lucky enough for her to stay in one spot and not roll all over the bed.

I'm not that lucky.

I kept holding onto her as I carefully leaned down to pull the comforter and sheet back in one fell swoop with my one not-so-free right hand. The pillow went in the opposite direction. I was just too emotionally and physically wasted to even care as I gently placed my heavy baby in her bed. She immediately rolled to her right side toward the wall. I picked up the pillow and gently raised her head. She breathed in a heavy sigh and then she was quiet. And still.

Whew. Who needs P90X? This 'lil gal is a workout all by herself.

I made it back to my room and attempted to fall asleep. The rolling started at 11:30ish. It had only been about an hour since I had put her down for the night. Right then I knew this was going to just be one of those nights. I rolled over and dragged my oh-so-weary legs over the side of the bed. *Get up, get up* I kept telling myself. I zombied on into her room again, into the doorway and past the play kitchen. DD is fast asleep in a position rivaled only by an employee of Cirque de Soleil. I stood there a minute and looked at her. How is she still asleep? I leaned in to pick her up. Lord knows she must have gained about one hundred *more* pounds since I was in here last. I picked her up from her pretzel nap and carried her into the bathroom. I stood her up, adjusted her clothes, and sat the Sleeping Giant on the toilet. Instinctively she uses it, in her sleep, and we zombie back into the room. I tuck her in for the third time. I make it back to my room and collapse in the bed and then...

The wrecking ball is back. I look over to that dreaded clock/radio. 4:24 am. My head started to hurt the instant my eyes opened. The monitor is glowing now and I hear, "Mommy...." I blinked and I was half the way there. In my haste I forgot that there were toys in the living room and I stepped on a big Lego block with that same still-half-asleep right leg/foot combo. Down goes Frazier with a quick upper cut. *I just broke my foot*, I thought. But none of that mattered because my baby needs her Mommy. I get to the bed and the contortionist has fashioned yet another exceptional position. The flailing is worse. *Maybe she's having a nightmare*, I thought.

I lean in to comfort her and almost get hit with a right. *Slow down Ali*, I thought to myself. I let out a little chuckle and DD's eyes opened. I shook my head in disbelief. She sat up in the bed and began to tell me everything that had happened in the last year. And just like that she was wide awake. Just like that. Un. Be. Lievable.

"ABBBA LEMMBO
TABBALABBA EEEDDD .....Mommy." she mumbled.

"You okay, Pumpkin?" I replied.

She put up her right hand and flashed the three-finger 'I LOVE YOU' sign and said "AH NUBB YEWWW....Mommy."

I kissed her face and said, "I love you, too baby." She laid her little head on the pillow and I tucked her in for the fourth time. I forgot that my foot was semi-broken. Crisis averted and all is well in the city. I zombied my way back to my room yet again.

In our first four years there were MANY nights just like this. Once my DM (dear mother) and I took turns holding her all night because she couldn't calm down enough to stay asleep. Any prolonged rousing would awaken her and there was no going back to sleep for at least an hour and a half. This plus her apnea makes for one zombie household. On one particular day I had taken her to therapy after one of these nights and the lack of sleep had gotten the best of me. In the waiting room I fought it for as much as I could, but the ride home was another story. About four miles from my house I stopped at a red light. I had no idea that I had fallen asleep until I woke suddenly and startled myself. I looked through the windshield. The light was still red. Two seconds later it turned green. That was the longest four miles of my life. We have had sleep studies, nasal sprays, ears checked, adenoids and tonsils removed, lavender scents, extra soft blankets, warm milk, nighttime rituals... You name it, we have done it. At times it was so bad I would just hold her, rock, and pray. At four years old she still slept only three to four hours at a stretch on a good night. Occasionally it would be five hours.

I don't worry over it now. It has become a part of my reality. I'm much less fettered by the why's and what if's and I'm long past feeling sorry for myself because I had a child born with a disability. On one occasion sitting in the therapist's waiting room I was having a pretty rough morning. Next to me was a fellow mom with the cutest little baby boy in a jogging suit. She was adjusting his clothes after putting on his shoe. She stood him up and pulled up his pant leg. I saw that the shoe had been put on a prosthetic and he only had one limb. This little munchkin seemed unbothered. He was just content with being cute. I thought to myself, "Why should I feel discouraged?" I think of him often. He should be at least seven or eight years old by now.

About an hour and a half later I felt a little hand on my face, poking at my eye. I opened them. Four inches from my face were two eyes and a megawatt smile. "Wannn Bee....NO-MAYYYYY?!?!" DD said. I looked at the clock/radio. 6:15 am. I closed my eyes. One little finger opened my eye and said again, "Wannn Bee....NO-MAYYYYY?!?!" The video 'Frozen' had been on while she slept. She asked, 'Wanna build a snowman?' She climbed into the bed and proceeded to reenact this scene between Anna and her sister. "UP UP!!!!" she insisted.

"Go away Anna," I said. "We live in Florida."

She laughed. I'm awake now.

She signs, "Breakfast?"

I look at the clock/radio. 6:30 am. Might as well. Time to make the doughnuts.

6

AN OPEN LETTER TO AN EXPECTANT SPECIAL NEEDS MOM

'Better to have it and not need it, then need it and not have it."' ~Mattie Henry

It's been a Friday that seemed more like Monday and I have been driving for over an hour and I'm STILL in the same city. Traffic was murderous at four o'clock and even worse at five. It has started to rain, I need gas, and the little person that is sitting behind me with headphones on is kicking the seat. The GPS keeps saying, *"...in one-tenth of a mile make a legal U-turn..."* My nerves are one step from shot but I WILL NOT BE DEFEATED. I'm going to make it to this conference tonight. I am determined. I looked in the rear view mirror and gave a side eye to DD. She knew what it meant. Stop kicking the seat, little girl.

About $12K in tolls later I had the destination in sight. I

pulled into the parking garage and circled to find a close space. DD has yet commenced to kicking the seat again. "Whew..." I thought as I turned the engine off. I gathered up DD's backpack and transferred a few snacks. I opened the door to the back seat and somebody was already out of the seatbelt, with a great big Kool-Aid smile on her face. All I could do was shake my head. Come on partner. Let's go.

I walked into the conference hall and stopped at the welcome desk. After getting my packet and name tag I headed into the main lobby. I saw familiar faces and we exchanged hellos. DD is with me and is working the crowd, ALREADY. I made my way to the hors d'oeuvres, made a plate for DD and I looked for a place to sit. I spotted an empty seat and another familiar face. I sat there...and then I saw you.

You were making your way over to the same seating area. Suddenly I didn't feel so tired. I smiled at you and asked, "Are you feeling okay?" You said, "Yes. About three weeks to go." with a smile and a rub to your stomach.

"Is this your first child?" I asked.

"No," you said, "I have two others. This child has Down

Syndrome and we came to the conference to get a little information. Trying to prepare, you know?"

You smiled at me. I smiled back and shook my head 'yes' in agreement. I knew very well. I knew VERY WELL.

After talking for a bit you told me that you were a speech therapist and that you knew sign language as well. My heart smiled more than my face ever could. 'You will need these skills' I thought to myself. I told you that you were doing a great thing in trying to learn as much as possible beforehand. "The best bit of advice that I can give you is to live for each moment because they will change", I said. Perhaps you knew what I meant. You will certainly find out very soon. I looked up and DD had yet again abandoned her chicken wings because there was music near. Before I knew it DD had hijacked the opening reception. You smiled and laughed with me. These moments are the ones that I speak of. Here are a few more nuggets of wisdom I have gathered over the years.

DON'T BE AFRAID TO CRY. There will be times that you cannot turn the faucet off. Don't try. Let those tears flow freely. They will give you strength that you didn't think that you had. These will not always be tears of sadness or of the unknown. They will change as your little one grows. Your tears are nothing to be ashamed of. We all have been there. Sometimes, I'm STILL there. Know that it is okay and don't ever let anyone tell you otherwise.

PARENT IN THE PRESENT. I notice that your name tag was pre-printed. You registered beforehand. There will be times when your BEST laid plans will be thwarted due to some unforeseen opponent that you may never discover. That's okay, too. Give your little one what he needs at the moment. Follow his lead. Be a hug ambassador. Make the rules as you go along. This journey will be more like your previous parenting experiences than not. The small nuances that set them apart may seem vast, but remember that your efforts will always benefit in some way...even if for a brief minute you may doubt yourself. Know that it's okay and don't let anyone tell you otherwise.

FAMILY DOESN'T ALWAYS MEAN FAMILY. You have been introduced to a unique class of individuals that many will never get to understand. There may be times that you feel misunderstood by blood relatives and friends alike. They may not understand why you cancel plans at the last minute or can't return a phone call promptly or couldn't go to a specific restaurant for dinner. Or why your phone has twelve specialists on speed dial. Or why you may get to a function late...or later than that. Trust that you have a new family of people that

GET IT. We understand everything and more without a word being said. Know that it's okay and don't let anyone tell you otherwise.

ACCEPT HELP. Your husband offered to take a photo of me and DD. Instinctively I said no at first, never wanting to 'bother' someone. I'm a culprit of this myself. YOU CAN'T DO IT ALONE. There are angels dispatched among us to help. LET THEM. They may not be in the form you may think. LET THEM. You will need them. LET THEM.

ENJOY THE RIDE. I sat next to you again the next day in one of the workshops. You seemed tired. Get ready. It's just beginning. Just know that this is the best tired you will ever feel. You'll be great. Don't let anyone tell you otherwise.

Welcome to the family, RK. Nice to meet you.

A version of this story was published on May 1, 2015 by The Mighty, an online community magazine designed to help those facing disease and disability.

Inclusion is for the Included

7

ABCs…AND IEPs

"Can't get blood out a turnip." ~Mattie Henry

The phone rings and breaks the much needed silence of what had been an already hectic day. I peered over to its resting place on the sofa and glanced at the Caller ID. XXXX ELEMENTARY 555-555-5555. *'Lord…what is it?'* I thought. There is always a sense of urgency for me when the school calls. All the tiredness that I felt went away by the second ring. I'm wide awake now.

"Hello…" I said.

"Hello…this is the Staffing Coordinator at XXXX Elementary. Is this the parent of DD?

"Yes. It is. How are you today?" My heart was still beating but now at a normal rhythm. I know she's not hurt. No trip to the campus for me.

"I'm okay. Thank you. Well Ms. Byrd I just wanted to let you know that we are going to have to change the date of the IEP meeting for DD again to accommodate the intern that administered her testing. She couldn't make the other date."

Silence. My mind is racing now. IEP. Intern. Testing. Date. Wait a minute.... intern???

"Are you there?" SC said.

"Yes...I'm here. What date are you thinking of? Let me get my planner." I replied. I'm glad that we weren't Skyping because I had a Scooby Doo type puzzled look on my face while I looked for my planner and a pen.

As it would be revealed, there was an intern that helped to administer some of the standard testing that my DD had earlier in the school year and she wanted to be present at the IEP meeting. Okay, I thought, but we had already changed the date of this meeting twice and this would be my third attempt at it. A few moments later, pen in hand, I wrote in a date that would be forever etched in my mind. Her IEP meeting had been set and my nerves were on edge. This is the big show. This would determine if the hard work that I had put in getting DD ready would be noticed. This would determine if she would be in an inclusive classroom. This is the prize fight and the purse is kindergarten. I said my goodbyes, set the phone on the charger and thought, *'Game on.'*

The next few weeks that passed were stressful to say the least. It was time for insurance renewals and finding out if we were cleared for continuation of care for DD's therapies has ALWAYS been a trying time at our household. This dance between doctors, therapists, insurance providers, and parents is an intricate one. One wrong step and we're sitting on the sidelines looking in. *No bueno.* But all parties kept the beat this time around and we continued busily on like we had been.

I had been gathering all of my supporting documents to take to the meeting as well as videos that I had taken of DD and posted on our FB page dedicated to our homeschooling journey. I talked to her therapists about attending and what questions I should ask concerning her goals. Her ST (speech therapist) and Feeding OT (occupational therapist) could not attend but gave great pointers. I wasn't happy that I would have to go alone but

I felt I was ready. I attended a state conference during that time which had a break-out session for IEP meetings which was SRO (standing-room-only) and heated. The parents looked dazed and confused. Some were a little angry. I listened to the information and my brain was racing. Did I really need an advocate or an attorney? How much was that going to cost? *'It can't be THAT bad,'* I thought, *'I'll highlight her strengths. I should be okay.'*

The day before IEP day was a Sunday. I went to the altar for prayer. And I left my burdens there. Don't pray and worry. I'm ready. I'm ready.

I sent DD to school on Monday and started to get ready. I pulled out a silk jade and brown pants suit. Not too subtle. Not too loud. A sneak attack type of power suit. I gathered my paperwork. I said one last prayer. I drove to the school, parked, and walked to the administration building. I signed in and sat down. I'm Money Mayweather. I've got this. I'm ready.

It took a few minutes for the staff to get ready. Apparently there was a need to print new testing results due to a few typos. Then I heard those words, "Ms. Byrd, we're ready for you." I picked up my packets and walked toward the room. This is it...FOR REAL.

I walked into the room and there were SEVEN, count 'em, one... two... three... four... five... six... SEVEN... people around a table looking at me. I scanned them all one-by-one. There were three people I had never seen. I guess it showed on my face. They began to introduce themselves. There was the SC (Staffing Coordinator), the school psychologist, a rep from AT (Assistive Technology), the school psychologist supervisor (SP), DD's current teacher and school ST (speech therapist) and a psychology intern. I zeroed in on the intern. I caught myself looking at her over my glasses. *'All right*, I thought, *let's get this party started.'*

Thirty minutes later we had gone over DD's evaluation and I took notes. I questioned the results of the testing in certain areas. I wanted to determine how the test was administered, not to be argumentative, but to be clear. I started firing off questions before I knew it. Did you spend any time with DD before you gave her the test? Did she seem comfortable with you? Where was the test given? Could any portion of it be modified? Do you know any sign language? Did she engage with you? The SP took over the answering session. I don't think that the intern anticipated much of what I was asking. But I thought this would be good for her. Let her cut her teeth on a mom like ME. I'll get you ready. You can bet on that.

An hour and a half had passed before I knew it. DD had joined us and was working the room. She wrote her name. She colored a picture...somewhat. She showed that the results of her testing did not adequately describe the person that she was. The air in the room had become a bit lighter. AT rep was VERY pleasant. She gave her observations of DD and her use of the school issued Ipad and was happy with her progress. She stated that this equipment would stay with her for class time and at home as well. The school ST concurred. They would hand-pick a teacher for her. I looked over and DD had crawled into the SP supervisor's lap. *'Way to work a room, kid'* I thought. Her current teacher had great input for DD's progress as well. Not surprising to me though. What teacher do you know that lets you SEND classwork TO the school? All the while SC was tapping on the keyboard and writing up the plan. At the two-hour mark I asked how much time would DD be in the classroom.

"100%." SC said. "That's what you wanted isn't it?" She passed a copy of the plan to me. I used my own pen and signed my name.

I smirked a little. "Sure is." I said as I passed the plan to AT. She passed to ST, and then intern, teacher, both SPs, and back to SC. DD had begun to 'teach' the people in the room from an empty space at the table. My heart was doing back flips. DD for the knock-out punch.

She would have a monitor for meals, continued speech and language, and help with reading and math. She would be in a General Education classroom. The LRE (least restrictive environment). She would go to school for a full day.

As we finished up I thanked each of them for the role they had played in helping us get to this point. "This could have been a fight, but it works a lot better if you are a TEAM. Thank you for not entering with a spirit of adversity." I told them. Then I told them about the blog. Evidence should always be substantiated, right?

I stepped out while the final copy was being printed and the intern passed heading for the door. I stopped her and asked how long it would be before she graduated. "I graduate in May", she said. She was in school at my graduate school alma mater. "You'll be just fine." I said to her with a smile and a nod. "Thank you." she said.

For five years I learned more abbreviations and acronyms than I cared to know: ST, OT, PT (physical therapy/therapist), AT, ESE (exceptional student education), VE-PreK (varying exceptionalities pre-kindergarten), VPK (voluntary pre-kindergarten), ESY (extended school year), H I J K L M N O P, two turtle doves and a partridge in a pear tree. IEP stands for 'Individualized Education Plan'. I had one as a gifted student. My DD has one as a student with exceptionality. The countdown has begun. August 24, 2015. Hello kindergarten. Here we come.

I stepped outside with my little one. I looked at her smiling face and asked, "Do you want to go celebrate? You're going to KINDERGARTEN!!!! Do you want to go get something to eat?" She looked up at me and signed, "BACON."

Gotta love her.

Inclusion is for the Included

8

TRAIN 'EM UP

"Can't plant squash and get collards." ~Mattie Henry

It's Monday morning. Day 4 of a four-day weekend and the house is in full morning swing. Breakfast, done. Breakfast dishes, done. I went outside to look over my garden with a little person hot on my heels. She plays in the play area with reckless abandon as I train the pea plants, all the while disbursing the mulch in the air to "Let It Go" from Disney's Frozen. I notice the delicate purple flowers and think to myself, *'It won't be long now.'* I look over and my DD has taken to the walkway near the side door and is looking back at me. She's five years old and has already perfected the side-eye. *'Sly little devil,'* I thought to myself. *'No escaping for you today. Time to go inside.'*

We walk into the house and I hear the phone ring. I look at the Caller ID. 'Transportation'. I answered with a reluctant, "Hello?"

"Good morning. Uh, Ms. Byrd? "

"Yes. This is she."

"Great. My name is YY ZZ. I am the Executive Area Director for AB County schools returning your call."

The wind just left my sails. So much for a blissful morning.

Last week was a short week for DD at school. Students had two days off with faculty preparing for report cards. With an already packed schedule I opted to change a few of DD's therapy appointments to the days she would be off from school and save myself the morning rush. As she entered the classroom I was greeted with a nervous smile from her kinder teacher. She informed me that DD had been having a few issues. Behavior issues.

'What NOW?!?!' I could only think as I listened.

She proceeded to tell me of an incident where DD had disrobed and come into the classroom and of another incident where she had run away from the class. Yet another incident in which she stayed in the bathroom too long and ignored the timer that rings after three minutes. What she said next made my face hot.

"...and I can't take time away from teaching other students to help her," she said.

I stepped closer. "And when did this happen?" I asked.

"Monday." She said.

I took another step towards her. Today is WEDNESDAY.

"And you didn't think enough to let me know some of these things when they happened? You need a PARA because you are OVER YOUR HEAD." I fumed.

I took a minute to breathe and realized that I had gotten REALLY close to her. I hugged my waist with my already crossed arms and took a big step back. I felt like I was playing an invisible game of 'Mother, May I.' I looked into the classroom for DD and she had done the usual morning things: put her backpack on the hook and gone to her seat. The other children were moving around in true kindergarten fashion.

All I could see was RED.

I turned to leave without as much of a goodbye. Speaking too much might have made me utter a few choice expletives that haven't been sanctioned by Webster's yet. I heard a voice as I turned to walk away saying, "Do you want to meet during the meeting next week or another time to discuss progress reports?"

I replied with, "Look in her planner. I wrote a reply yesterday."

I left the school that day as upset as I had ever been. I was already teetering on the brink of going back to homeschooling and this was the proverbial nail in the coffin. So rather than make a rash decision I sat down and began to write. And call. And write some more. And leave voice messages. And ask for an emergency IEP meeting.

And pray. And pray some more.

Today I got a reply. That was Wednesday. Today is Monday. And all I want to do is tend my garden and not think about the school because today she is at home with me. No acting under duress. No pull outs or reprimands. Today she is with me. And I just want to tend my garden.

But now I need to tend to the issue at hand. And I'm ready.

"This is a call I was not expecting." I told Ms. ZZ. "I called the Superintendent of Schools and was directed to the Regional Director for my area and then to another coordinator that I had already spoken to before. Where do you fall in this lineup?"

She replied, "I'm second to the regional Director."

I felt a little better. I had long been tired of talking to Indians. Right now I needed a Chief. I had meetings with the teacher, principal, an advocate, an attorney and a friend who was a staffing specialist and I was about all talked out. But I put my own personal grief with the situation on the shelf because now DD needs me. And I must deliver.

I went on to tell Ms. ZZ of the frustration that I felt about the school system as a whole in relation to children with special needs. It makes absolutely no sense the obstacles that families face in pursuit of the quality education our children are entitled to. The system fails us in its feeble attempts at inclusion. It helps to the point of hindering. If you are not a hard-nosed advocate you will surely get swept away into a tide of pull outs, and push-ins, and IEPs, and school-supported therapies. Our children are turned every which way but loose in a whirlwind of 'neededness' by individuals who are ill-equipped to teach the WHOLE child yet rally to the rescue for the disability. You may be a GREAT candidate on paper but not necessarily the best fit for the child. Knowing is half the battle. The problem that I face is that they know it, but have not done much to rectify the problem besides push paper. All the while the days turn into weeks and the weeks into months. And the months into regression. Then we have to start all over. Aggressively.

Right now I'm sick to my stomach of hearing 'she needs' or 'she does/doesn't qualify for' and all her progress report shows is that she needs to work on skills or that she is below level.

DD is not her disability. She is my daughter. She CAN and not because the school has helped her. It has been ten weeks into kindergarten. And that has been ten weeks too many because in this time I have not seen one definitive skill that she has learned. I know that this takes an adjustment period and I'm not jaded. I am fully aware that she is not a rocket scientist as of yet but I need to see something that she has done. And not only hear about the CAN'T or the negative things she did. I have proof that she can do much more than she is given credit for.

And I'm not the only parent that feels this way.

Ms. ZZ took note of all my points, both subtle and blatant, and assured me that my next IEP meeting the coordinator would surely be in attendance to get DD the scheduling that would best suit her and help her to thrive in an inclusive environment. I thanked her for listening.

As I hung up I felt a tug at my leg and looked down. There was a little person holding a cup up to me. She said,

"Zeus." Loose translation: JUICE. Suddenly I wasn't thirty-eight hot. Well, maybe still simmering around twelve or thirteen. I looked down into those almond-shaped eyes and remembered why I go so hard. She's DD. My dear daughter. And I'm her mom. Her biggest advocate. I go hard like a red-nosed pit. I don't let go. And I think the powers that be know it.

I go into the kitchen and the juice is already on the counter. I smile and pour up the Welch's. I look through the window and see my garden. I look for the purple flowers and think about the peas. You have to train them to grow up a pole; otherwise they fall and do not produce much. I gave my little pea her juice and she said, "Tank Que".

I wasn't worried about the garden outside anymore. I had a little pea right beside me that needed tending.

Gotta train 'em, you know?

9

STOP THE R-WORD

'Talk about me as much as you please. The more you talk I'm gonna bend my knees.' ~Gospel Song

It's Saturday and in forty-five minutes DD needs to be suited up, helmet on, mounted and in the arena. Her private horseback riding lesson starts at 1 pm. It's 12:40. I'm ten minutes away. And this light has changed on me three times already. There are at least six cars ahead of me and this light allows for three to pass before the yellow flashes and maybe one more. If the car in front of me is with it, I am too. I checked. No intersection red light camera. I'm all in. I'm about to run this bad boy.

Somebody should have told the car two cars ahead of us not to sleep at the light. The whole line missed the turn. Now I have to wait another cycle. City planners did a HORRIBLE job with the traffic control in this new suburb.

The stables are far on the outskirts of the city in a newly minted community to the west of EVERYTHING. The homes are large. The lots are small. The taxes are plentiful. The traffic is congested. There is just enough of the original countryside left to remain rural-ish and at the next intersection there is an outside wondermall of contemporary stores, restaurants, and other shopping venues. No need to travel beyond your neighborhood. They are pretty well self-contained complete with McDonald's and Target and a full parking lot with tiny spaces filled with mammoth SUVs.

I look in the rear view mirror between breaths of frustration and find DD fast asleep, head reared back and mouth open. 'I have a good mind to turn around and go home' I thought. But that wouldn't be the thing to do because she woke up EARLY signing 'horses Mommy' and clapping her tiny hands. I love to see her happy and I'll forge the ends of the Earth and combat this treacherous traffic to see that toothy grin. Had it been any other day, though.... GUESS WHAT?!?!?

I lifted my head from its perch on my left-windowsilled arm prop and looked ahead. The light was about to change again. I looked at the console: 12:50 pm. 'If these people pay attention I can make it' I thought to myself. The cars began to move. One car, two cars, the third car on two wheels. By Joe I think I'll make it. As I got closer the light turned yellow. 'Not today' I said under my breath. I checked the rear view and DD rolled her head with the turn. STILL asleep. Now if only she would sleep like this at night. That would be a miracle. What is really going to be the miracle is if I make it to the stables in ten minutes. I moved into a free lane on the straightway and opened up the V-12. Leggo.

The traffic gods must have heard my frustration because at 12:58 I rolled up to the gate. I pulled in as far as I could off the road and opened the door. I jumped down from the driver seat and pressed the gate button. I could hear the motor gears turning as the gate slowly began to recoil. DD.... STILL asleep. I jumped back into the SUV and reached through the middle. Her little head moved as I shook her leg. "Time for horses, Toot!" I said. Her little groggy eyes opened wide when she realized where we were and in the snap of a finger she was alert and anxious, happily clapping, and ready for what was next. I passed through the opened gate and up the driveway to the tack house. I pulled into an empty space next to a white SUV with a little girl sitting on the back under its lifted door. As I glanced at the console I felt a sigh of relief. 1:00 pm. I made it.

We exited my SUV and walked into the tack house. I

located the helmet with the short chin strap and guided DD to the adjacent couch. Pink cowboy boots, ON. Helmet, ON. We headed through the middle door into the stables and walked past those magnificent animals in the hay. These thoroughbreds stood much taller than we and the splendor they emitted shone as brightly as the calm in their spirit. They glanced at us with those caring eyes as if to say 'Hello. Welcome back". Halfway through we saw her instructor clad in jeans and a straw hat and boots afoot.

"Good afternoon DD!" she said. "Are you ready to ride?"

DD responded with a resounding "YAY!!!" as she jumped in place and reached for the reigns.

The white horse that she would ride was named Patrick. He was an old pony with a mild temperament that all the little ones began with. He shed something fierce and at the end of each lesson DD needed as much brushing as they gave him in the grooming stall. I didn't mind though. Just to see her in the arena pulling left and turning right with those reigns in her hand and a smile on her face was enough to make me forget about that rug she ended up with. Boy, could Patrick shed...even when he was groomed and his coat shorn. He didn't seem to care. So why should I?

They exited the stables and DD greeted each horse on the way out. "HI!" she said, excitedly waving and walking Patrick to the mounting area. A wonderfully brown thoroughbred with a shiny black mane leaned over his gate and responded with a majestic whinny, the sound most often heard when horses are separated from one another or when horses closely bonded see each other after separation. Did he recognize this little creature with the cute pink boots? Only he would know. She smiled back and pointed. "Horse" she said and signed with her free left hand.

A few more steps and they left the stables, walking Patrick to the stand where DD would climb up to mount. She was still too short to climb over even on the top step but that didn't stop her. A little boost from the instructor was all she needed. Squarely in the saddle she put her feet in the stirrups and grabbed the reins by the braid. A quick 'kick, kick' and the trio were off to the arena. I snapped a quick picture as I exited stage left to sit under the gazebo and wait while she had her lesson. I found a spot to sit as I watched the pink boots get farther and farther away.

About forty minutes later they began to come back toward the stables. I had been joined by the driver of the white SUV and her daughter as I waited. Her other daughter was riding in the closer ring. She didn't say much. As a matter of fact, she didn't say anything at all. 'Does she see me sitting there?" I thought. In my mind I could hear my grandmother saying that some people just aren't friendly and if people don't want to be bothered, don't bother them. This I knew. It's sad but some things you just get used to. DD never meets a stranger. I like that about her. She's a honey drop in a world of vinegar. I'll take sweet over sour any day. I had no idea that the sour was on the way.

They headed toward the gazebo and past the stables into a grooming stall in back of where the horses were housed. I stood and directed a friendly smile toward my gazebo mates. She looked back with an acknowledging glance and was back to her activity. I could see her in my periphery as they left the gazebo a few minutes after I did. We went in opposite directions but I saw them again as I walked to the back grooming stall where DD was busily hosing Patrick down and brushing his coat.

White SUV walked over to the instructor and started talking. A lot. Matter of fact more than she should have during another child's lesson.

Did she not see me standing there?

She went on to explain that she would have to change her daughter that rides' lesson to another day because of some issue at school. She rattled on and on about this and that and then more this and that as her other daughter played in the grooming area. The instructor was trying to be cordial, but the distraction was getting the best of DD, and it was becoming hard to keep her focused. Now DD was jumping in the puddles. Then DD started picking up the spray bottles. Then she tried to go under Patrick. I could see that we were headed toward a complete loss of attention here. White SUV was STILL talking.

This is supposed to be DD's lesson. You can wait your turn White SUV.

I stepped in to help regain DD's focus but the other child in the grooming area signaled a time to play and the calm that the previous lesson generated went straight out the door.

White SUV was STILL talking.

Now she had to recount her whole driving experience on the way to the stables. I understood because I had my own stressful trip there as well; but right now wasn't the time that I needed to hear about it. And if that wasn't good enough, she said,

..."and I don't know WHY I even went that way because the traffic is SOOO bad. I'm such a RE-TARD!"

Inclusion is for the Included

Okay dammit. This has gone on long enough. Stop the world. I'm about to straighten White SUV. I swear I felt a shift in the rotational axis. I walked toward White SUV and interrupted her ever continuing conversation with the instructor. She was talking so much she didn't even see me coming until I was right in front of her.

"Excuse me...can I talk to you for a minute?" I asked.

"Yes?..." she said hesitantly. I walked off to the side. Her daughter walked behind her.

"Alone. Without your daughter." I said. "I don't want her to hear what I'm about to say."

White SUV told her daughter to stay where she was as she followed me to a more secluded side. I looked over at my daughter and how happy she was. My brown skin was boiling but you would never know it because right now I was as smug as a world class poker player. You'll never know just how mad I am until I need to let you know. And right now I was about to unleash the educated beast.

"I just listened to you talk on and on about things and something you said REALLY bothered me." I said.

White SUV looked puzzled.

"You were talking and I heard you use the R-word. Do you

not see my daughter standing over there? She has Down syndrome. Do you think that was an appropriate comment to make where she can hear you? And in front of *your* daughter?"

White SUV was still puzzled. She said, "Oh I didn't mean it like that," she said casually.

"Well when you make comments like that openly they are hurtful and mean and you shouldn't say things that will upset other people." I said.

White SUV was STILL puzzled. She said, "Oh...well...I didn't mean to upset you. I was just talking about my day. My nephew is autistic."

WELL DAMN.

I just felt the world shift onto the opposite axis. If I had a clue, I would give it to her. NO CHARGE. Clearly she missed the whole, entire, complete, and unmitigated point.

"Well...for future reference I'd think about finding another word to describe yourself." I said.

White SUV gave a quick 'well, whatever look' and motioned for her daughter to join her. She told the instructor that she would talk to her later as she walked away. By this time, I was seething and I just wanted to get away from there and take my baby home and away from this negativity. I told the instructor that I would call the next week if we needed to change the lesson time because DD had choir rehearsal at the church. She obliged as she gave DD a hug and told her she'd see her next week.

"Byeeee!" DD waved gleefully as she reached for my hand. We walked away, heading toward the front of the stables where my car was parked. The white SUV was still in the same parking space and the little girl was once again sitting on the back under the lift gate. I walked over to the passenger side and opened the door for DD. I helped her into her booster seat and strapped her in. She waved at the little girl and said "Byeeee!" with the enthusiasm of an Olympic athlete who just won his event. The little girl looked over at DD, then at me, then back at DD. Hesitantly she waved back but said nothing.

I closed the door with a resounding thud as DD picked up her headphones and put them on her head. I opened the driver's door and climbed into my seat. I closed the door and reached for the ignition. I could see DD as she happily watched the movie playing in the headrest as I turned the key over. The roar of the engine felt good to my body as the pistons fired away seemingly taking all the energy I had expended on a hopeless cause and using it for their own good. I could feel the calm cover over me again. I took a few breaths and reached for the gear shift. As I put the SUV in reverse I could see DD in the rear view mirror looking at me. "French fries, Mommy," she signed, all the while not missing a second of her movie. I looked back and responded to her reflection with a smile and shook my head 'Yes'. She did a little dance in the seat and went back to the movie. The wheels rolled back and I left my space next to the white SUV and as I shifted into drive I could see White SUV in the distance under the gazebo. As I drove away the thought of my last conversation became less daunting and by the time I pressed the button to open the gate it was a non-factor. I make a quick right onto the main road and headed toward the french fries. Anything to make her smile. Anything.

I often think about that encounter. It was one of the first times I had ever had to educate a person on the use of a derogatory and demeaning word such as this. The R-word cuts like a double-edged sword. It pierces my heart and my head simultaneously. It's hurtful on all fronts. It's a slap in the face. It's a stab in the back. It's used interchangeably with the purposeful and the irreverent, the playful and the condescending, the noun, the verb, and the adjective. Never has one word set in place so many emotions in my life as this one. It hurts even more when you speak up and the action is just deemed dismissive.

There were so many variables to that choice encounter. The fact that she at first never even acknowledged the fact that neither my daughter nor I were even in the universe was the first flag. Her having a disability was just icing on the cake. It takes nothing to speak to someone. Hellos are free and plentiful. I remember being told as a child to 'go and make a friend'. We expect children to be forward and accepting but somewhere in the divide between childhood and becoming an adult the concept gets lost in the shuffle. We don't meet strangers. There have been several times that we have been places and spoken to someone, not knowing that they were having a bad day. We unknowingly made these people happy and they told us so. Those are the gifts the universe grants us if we are willing to exude the energy and positivity they require. Common sense, however, isn't so common.

Secondly, casually spouting on and on about any range of topics is rude in certain arenas. Even though the atmosphere was relaxed the time that we were there had a price. It belonged to DD and the benefit of that time would prove fleeting if the interruptions continued. I didn't want to meet rude with rude but sometimes taking the moral high road can prove to serve more harm than good. And what's more she saw absolutely nothing wrong with doing so.

This leads to perhaps the most interesting segue: if she was so comfortable using the R-word, what other words would so casually roll from her lips? When would another woman become a B, or a racially motivated expletive, or any other derogatory phrase used to demean and degrade? And what do we teach our children by doing so in front of them? They learn what they see. They can only learn what they are taught. They are sponges that soak up every essence we emit, whether good or bad, and hold onto those life lessons until such time presents itself that they might be used. We are given a charge to be good stewards over everything that we are given. That includes our children. They are the most precious gift from God we could ever possess save the breath we take. We must take care as parents to guide them through this life and become good stewards themselves.

Many will say it's much ado about nothing. It's just a word. Words can't do anything. But I fiercely beg to differ. Speaking up about the R-word took more confidence than I knew that I had. It is uncomfortable to tell a grown person that they are wrong. The recipient has two options: accept or reject. In my instance, well, I guess it was a rejection, but the insolence and dismissive air that surrounded the whole situation could not be easily described. What I will admit, however, is that I owned each action. Those feelings were MINE and I OWNED them. What WHITE SUV did with them was left up to her, but I had confidence in knowing that I did the right thing, whether it was received or not. I took a stand. I did it. I really did it.

As parents of children with special needs we are called to action in almost every instance of our lives. Whether for business or pleasure we encounter those who will embrace us and in the same breath take ours away. What will we do with these teachable moments? Will we rise to the occasion or set it aside for another day? Will we assert our disdain with boldness or will we silently sulk? There is no right or wrong answer. Our tears can prove just as empowering as the words we craft so eloquently to slay a harm-spewing opponent. We must take each instance in stride and do what our hearts deem right. When we learn better we must do better. It is our moral obligation to do so. And what's more, by acknowledging that the things we say may and will hurt someone adversely is part of being a grown up. It's no affront to your person to say, 'I'm sorry' and after that apology vow to do better. Much better.

It has been a year since we have been to the stables for private lessons. DD's scheduling did not permit much wiggle room for extras after beginning kindergarten and I didn't press the issue. Perhaps the thought of running into

White SUV again was a bit much for me. Who's to say? DD takes therapeutic riding lessons now. The staff at the center are the most warm, kind, and accepting people. We choose them. But in that choosing do not think that we ran from the thought of a possible confrontation. We chose the love. We chose the smiles. We chose the waves from the stables and the hugs at the gate. We chose to smile and not to frown. One bad apple CAN spoil the whole bunch but in this case we just chose not to eat apples anymore.

We choose French Fries.

Inclusion is for the Included

10

PINK AND YELLOW AND BLUE

"Every round goes higher and higher..."
~Baptist Hymn

There are pink ribbons everywhere. Men wear pink ties and runners pink tutus. The car in front of me at the red light has a pink license plate holder. The beauty supply store has a pink blow dryer and flat iron set that benefits a national foundation. I feel a cooler breeze on my skin and there are more leaves adorning the once green grass that is my back lawn. It is October. The beginning of fall. The season of pumpkin this and spiced that.

Yet amidst the rustic autumn colors and a vast sea of pink I see a festive splash of yellow and blue from a familiar face on my Facebook timeline with a moniker I have grown accustomed to seeing: *more alike than different.* As I scroll I see another stating, *'I rock an extra chromosome.*

What's your superpower?' The advocates are out in full force spreading facts in attempts to bring awareness and shatter stereotypes. But this time it's not about pink. October is Down Syndrome Awareness Month.

I became a mother on a windy Wednesday morning in January of 2010. I became an advocate some time later. I became a super mom in the next year and took my spot back as Alpha in the year after that. I channeled my hurt and despair for the unknown into advocacy and work for my dear daughter (DD). The last two years have been a whirlwind and I have powered through them with all the strength I could find left in my reserves. I am a special needs mom. That's my super power. I have become sensitive and insensitive, afraid and courageous, strong and uncontrollably inconsolable, all while embracing this journey less travelled by those who seldom choose this path yet are chosen just the same. It's October again. October is Down Syndrome Awareness Month.

I scroll and see another post from a friend whose daughter just got accepted to COLLEGE. The fact that she has Down Syndrome is just a sweet addition to the news. Barriers are being chiseled away. It does my heart proud to see this because when DD is able to apply for college a decade or so from now the foundation would have already been laid. We are on the verge of our second IEP meeting for kindergarten. The pangs of inclusion tug fiercely at my heart and I go to bat for her with no holds barred. She CAN and she WILL. And not just in October but every day.

Each year I reflect on myself and how far we have come. In similar fashion I also am sorely aware that we have further to go. Awareness comes at a price. Sometimes steep. Sometimes amicable. Sometimes steady and sometimes fluctuating. Yet we are thoroughbreds. We attack the curves just as we breeze the straightaways. October brings about a chance for me to assess my own journey. I revel in the days that are light and airy and I feel as though my course is plain and in the next instant I am engulfed in fog. It is a non-stop bullet train with the highest peaks and the lowest valleys and we hold on for our non-stop lives. I am a special needs mom. It's what I do. I hold on. And then I hold on some more.

In these short five and a half years I have become more aware than I ever thought I could be. Self-aware. Aware of my surroundings. Aware of those looks, those stares, those eerie moments when a complete stranger looks for the right way to approach you. I am also aware that there are great people who understand what you feel without saying a word. I know now that family is not totally a blood standard but moreover a collection of venerable souls who love you for the familiarity you bring. So rather than post for others I remember a few mantras that help me get through the rough patches.

CURIOSITY CAN LEAD TO ADVOCACY. Take a moment to remind someone that we are all people first. Conditions are just that - conditions. They are simply the extra that makes us human. So if you can stare you should be able to share. Help someone say 'Hi' and they may say 'Hi' back.

EMBRACE YOUR INNER VELOCIRAPTOR. Don't be afraid to take a note from these seemingly unassuming creatures. Sometimes you just have to tap your claw to let a naysayer know you mean business. Some people can be downright mean...on purpose. Others can try and sugar coat an insult with, "But I didn't mean it that way". These are the times that you may have to go Jurassic Park on them and then put your claws away for another day. Let them know that you can be fierce if need be and kind the next, but all the while gaining the respect that is due.

YOUR NEW LIFE IS FOR THE LIVING. I have come to realize that the life I once led is no more. I still have my memories but I don't long for those days. I have found a new sense of self in the life that I have now. I do not tread on rose petals most days but when I do the fragrance they emit is the most sweet and savory that I have ever smelled. The road I travel has narrow alleys but they are lined with interesting nuances I would have never otherwise seen on a wide open path. I am well aware that I must trust my instincts and parent in the present. I kiss her little face, she kisses me back and I'm alive inside. I am a special needs mom. It's who I am. It's what I do.

It's October again. I think I'll hold on to this new life and live it up. Then I'll hold on some more.

If you would like to donate to Team Purple Pyramid for Step Up for Down Syndrome, visit our page at www.stepuporlando.kintera.org/purplepyramid or directly in our name to the Down Syndrome Association of Central Florida.

Inclusion is for the Included

11

SUPER TUESDAY

'Everything'll be alright...else it'll be all wrong.'
~Mattie Henry

I checked the clock. 8:07 am. I have roughly twenty minutes to get the little girl that lives in my house dressed, hair done, and out of the door. Will I make it? Heaven only knows. I was trying to wait her out until she was finished eating but we were running short on minutes and needed to get a move on. I have everything laid out next to me on the couch: lotion, underwear, outfit, shoes and socks, hair bows, brush, comb, spray bottle. My oh my – this little girl has a glam squad getting her ready for kindergarten. It's a good thing that her mommy is a stylist because this level of suitin' and bootin' is reserved for those who regularly walk a red carpet. You couldn't tell her that, though. The world is her stage and she rips the runway with much 'tude.

The television is on and Scooby Doo is helping to solve the latest mystery along with his meddlesome compadres. It is an ongoing war that we wage: to Doo or not to Doo. This battle went to DD as she sat and finished her breakfast. As I maneuvered behind her I could hear another television just behind the wall. The presidential candidates are in a fierce war of words trying desperately to outdo each other with clever witticisms. Pundits are all so eager to opine and sip on airtime. 'Humph...' I thought to myself. 'The campaign trail has nothing on our household. Forget the race to the White House. The real race is getting out of MY house.' I checked the time again. 8:15 am. I was still fairly on schedule. I had given myself ten minutes to finish her hair and load the SUV. So far so good.

I picked up the spray bottle and aimed it at her hair. I shook my head as I brushed away the grits from the remnants of what was once a bed-head ponytail. This little girl tickles me. A few quick sprays of water and like magic her curls reform. I pick up a brush and smooth one puff, then two, then one double-ponytail, then two. A few twists and barrettes on the ends and we are done. 8:23 am. I tap her on the shoulder and she turns to look at me. "Let's go Toot." I say. She picked up the remaining bacon on her orange sectioned plate. She headed to the kitchen with plate in hand as I headed to that place behind the wall where I hear the candidates' voices. I glance at the television as I put on my shoes and shake my head again. I can still hear them as I walk away from the room and toward the front door.

Meanwhile DD has gathered every toy imaginable in attempts to take them with her and has not remotely even thought that she might, maybe, or perhaps need her backpack. "We don't need those today. Leave them here for when you get back." I tell her but she is not having it. We finally compromised on a pink plastic plate with Minnie Mouse in the center just to get her out the door. I picked up the previous night's homework from the cubicle by the door along with the backpack that she refused to acknowledge this morning: 8:30 am. I am now officially running late. Thank you, Minnie Mouse. Thank you.

I try to give her the backpack but she won't even look at it much less put it on her back. I feel like it's going to be one of those days again as I turn the lock on the door and pull it closed. I hear the faint click behind me as it locked and we walk toward the driveway. DD is unphased and her personal assistant is closely afoot with bags and keys in tow. Shifting hands to free the SUV keys from their hiding place under the backpack and homework I press the transponder on the unlock button. Nothing. I press it again. Nothing. DD is striking poses for her shadow oblivious that her mom can't get the door open. I press and wriggle my finger and I hear the familiar click of the front doors unlocking. I try again. Nothing. I shake my head again. 'Another thing to deal with this morning,' I thought. I tried the button one last time and I heard the second click of the back doors unlocking. I exhaled and turned to get DD's attention.

"Time to go to school, Toot."

"No." she said as she turned back to dancing with her shadow.

I had to call on the Father, the Son, the Holy Ghost and ten thousand angels to gather myself as I opened the back passenger door. The door handle gave way and freed itself from the place it had resided since the vehicle was purchased. I shifted the cargo in my arms once again and gently opened the door as best I could. The cargo held a much different fate, however. I threw the backpack, my purse, and the homework in the SUV. I turned toward DD, who now has her hands on her hips and is a dance-off with her shadow, oblivious that the clock is ticking and her mother is too.

"Toot, LET'S GO!!!" I shout as I walk toward her. She spins on a dime; hand on hips, and Minnie Mouse plate in the free hand. She bops toward the SUV and stops again at the open door.

"Get in, Sweet. We're late for school." I say.

'No." she said again.

I lean down to pull her up onto the running board. She is stiff as a board and doesn't want to get in. I pick her legs up and scoot her into the back seat in one motion. Before she could turn around I had closed the door on her, the backpack, the homework, my purse AND Minnie Mouse and was headed to the other side of the SUV. I opened the driver's door and climbed into the seat. I put the key in the ignition and turned the vehicle on. The roar of the engine was powerful yet calming. We were FINALLY leaving the house. I checked the rear view mirror. DD is sitting NEXT TO her booster seat and smiling a big snaggled-toothed grin.

"Get in your seat, Toot..." I say. I'm already exhausted and I haven't left the driveway.

"Get in the seat." she replies, giggling and she climbs into the booster.

I opened the door and walked to the back passenger door again. I couldn't believe that I had forgotten to buckle her in. Well...yes I could. Right then I would have forgotten my own name. A quick click and a kiss on her cheek and I returned to the front seat. I buckled myself in and looked at the clock. 8:36 am. The morning bell rings at 8:35 am. Late isn't even the word. As a matter of fact, this is what can be called normal on any given day in our household.

I say my prayers as I back out of the driveway. I check the rear view mirror and DD has turned on the DVD player in my headrest and put on her headphones. I can hear Scooby Doo as we ride toward the exit to the subdivision and onto the main street. The headphones are too loud but that is a battle I'll have to reserve for another ride because I have less than ten minutes to get her to school, unloaded, and walked to class. I don't think I'll make it today, not without a minor miracle. Maybe I shouldn't have said my prayers in a hurry. I need them to pull through right now. A short mile later and I stop at a stop sign and I hear, "DING DING DING!!!"

I look at the digital dashboard. FUEL LEVEL LOW.

At this point all I can do is laugh. I chuckled to myself and I thought about all the things that I needed to do after I dropped DD at school that did not include a trip to the gas station. Nonetheless, a quick jaunt around the next corner and the entrance gate was in full view. I slowly drove over two speed humps and made a left onto the campus. Following the circular road way, I bypassed the parking lot and pulled up to the curb right near the yellow 'no parking' line. I checked the time again: 8:42 am. I've got three minutes to make it happen. I turned off the SUV and reached between the seats to the backpack on the floor. DD took her headphones off and tossed them on the floor underfoot.

"Don't put those headphones on the floor. You'll step on them and break them, Toot." I said to oblivious ears as I leaned a little farther and unbuckled her seatbelt.

She turned to open the door as I got out and met her on her side. She stood in the door and lunged onto me as I stood in front of her. She has not a care in the world, confident that I will be there to catch her. Her little arms are tightly wound around my neck and I feel something pressed against my ear. I lift her onto the ground and look in her hand: It's that Minnie Mouse plate. I reach for the plate that she reluctantly hands over and set it on the booster seat to much protest.

"Leave Minnie here for when you come home. She'll see you after school. Tell her bye-bye." I said.

"Bye bye Mi Moussss..." she said as I helped her arms through her backpack. I handed her the homework and grabbed my phone. We headed toward the gate.

A short walk past two opened doors and we were at her classroom. She walked in and looked around. After a quick greeting from one of her classmates, she took her backpack off and hung it on the hook under her personal cubby. The teacher walked toward me as I watched DD.

"Good morning," I said. "She's having quite a day."

The teacher replied with a smile saying, "It's okay. We all have those mornings."

DD had joined her classmates on the carpet for morning story time. I looked at her happy face as she found her assigned space and sat between the children who were already seated. It makes me proud to see her assimilate herself into the classroom culture. With all of the problems we have had to get to this point seeing her happy in this space makes me feel more confident about keeping her in public school. It's a daily struggle, though. For as much as I am happy about her days the reservations I have are just as numerous. I took a deep breath in and waved good bye as I exhaled and turned to walk away.

A quick exit stage left and I was on the walkway, past the two open doors, and headed back to the SUV. I heard the bell sound. I had made it with only a few seconds to spare. I met another mom with a cute little girl in tow. I thought to myself, 'I'm not late if someone shows up after me' and let out a tiny audible chuckle. The mom smiles back and offers a pleasant, "Good morning." I reply with, "Good morning" and round the corner of the SUV, open the door, and climb in.

I checked my phone as I sat in the drivers' seat. One missed call, two new emails, and a Facebook notification. I plugged the phone into the car charger and turned on the engine. The radio station has gone to commercial break and the morning anchor is urging all who listen to exercise their right to vote. I listen and reply to the voice I hear through those Bose speakers, "I'm already with ya, sister".

Today is Super Tuesday. It is 8:50 am and this super mom is already super tired. At least I didn't have to travel far because the community center that I was to frequent to cast my ballot was next door to the school. Game point, match set. Let's get this show on the road...if I don't run out of gas first.

I round the circular driveway carefully. The car loop is a dangerous place this time of morning. The late are rushing oblivious of others and noncompliant with the posted speed. There can easily be a catastrophe if you do not pay swift attention to your surroundings. I just feel bad for the children. About a week ago I saw two parents get into a shouting match because one parent didn't move her car up as far as the other thought she should. It looked like McEnroe and the judge at Wimbledon. And in their shouting they held up a whole line of other cars. I was just glad to be driving AWAY from the loop and starting my own day.

All of two minutes later I was turning in to the community center parking lot. There were signs that directed voters where to park and I followed them to a space close to the back door where we would enter the polling place. I backed into a space and gathered my purse. I searched for my passport, took it out, and replaced the purse on the floor in the back seat. I climbed out of the SUV and walked toward the smart looking older gentleman that stood before the polling center door.

"Good morning. Please have your driver license ready for the worker as you enter." he said.

I smiled and said, "Good morning" as I opened my passport and looked for my drivers' license in its usual place. It wasn't there. I thought to myself, 'did I leave it in my purse?' as I searched through the cards that were tucked into the side pockets. 'I might have taken it out when I went to the DMV the other day and not put it back,' I said to myself as I finally spotted a familiar barcode and pulled the white card from behind another tucked into the passport. I handed it to the gentleman.

"Do you have a driver license?" he said to me.

I gave him a puzzled look as I reached for the card he handed to me: DD's insurance card. I just shook my head.

"Yes. I do." I said as I put the card back into the side pocket. I took out all the cards stashed in the passport on that side and checked them one-by-one. My driver's license was at the back, turned around, with the barcode exposed. That's why I hadn't seen it immediately. I took it out and gave it to him.

"Give it to the poll worker after you enter." he said as I entered the polling place. I bet that's first for him. Who gives an insurance card instead of a license? Short answer: ME! I stepped behind the red line and waited my turn. One of the ladies at the table motioned for me to come forward and I handed her my license. There was a bowl of the good peppermint on the table and I helped myself to a few. These were the kind that melted when you put them in your mouth. I popped one in my mouth as I waited. The poller was taking a little time to find my name. She asked if my name and address was current and correct on the license, to which I answered, 'Yes'. She turned to the lady sitting next to her and asked her a question. I picked up another peppermint. I love these things. I popped another one in my mouth.

The poller turned back to me and said that she couldn't find my name on the roster. A million things were going through my head as I thought about all the tactics that my predecessors had to endure just to vote, some of which were still being put into practice today only in more covert ways. She instructed me to come over to a side kiosk where another worker would help me find my correct polling place. A few questions and a lagging server later I was instructed to sign my name verifying that I was given said information and told where to go to cast my ballot. They offered directions to which I respectfully declined. I had gone to this polling place before and knew the way. As I left I tried to jog my foggy memory to recall if I had received any mail to support my polling place being changed. I couldn't remember for the life of me if I had. I climbed back into the SUV and was on my way to the next polling place two miles away. I know those workers got a kick out of my story that morning. Oh well...follow the yellow brick road.

Five minutes, three stop signs, and a roundabout later I was at the next polling place. It was a church in my neighborhood that I had voted at before. There were no sign wielding, flag waving, honk-your-horn-for-us volunteers on the road. If I didn't already know it was an election day I wouldn't have even realized it. I turned onto the church parking lot and there I saw it. There was one sign perched a regulation one hundred feet from the church building. Only one sign. One lone sign. One single solitary campaign sign on church property. I passed by it and found a parking place in the empty parking lot. I got out and aimed my camera for a quick photo. I checked the photo and took another. 'This is sad' I thought as I walked toward the double doors.

As I got closer to the building I noticed that I was being watched. I greeted the poll worker with a fond 'Good morning' before I asked her about having campaign sign posted on church property. She directed me to the poll manager just inside the next set of double doors. She asked if that was why I took the pictures. "Yes. It is." I replied.

I entered the polling place, which also doubled as the main sanctuary, and walked over to the poller who took my driver license and proceeded to search for me in the system. The poll manager was sitting next to her. I asked her about having the campaign signs posted on church property.

"As long as it is one hundred feet away from the building," she said.

"But the building is a church. According to the separation of church and state can a campaign sign be legally posted on church property?" I asked. "I was thinking that the signs could be posted on the easement along the street because that is city property. Once you turn into the parking lot it becomes church property and would therefore constitute an endorsement. I've voted here before and I have NEVER seen a campaign sign anywhere on church property."

The poll manager looked dumbfounded. Crickets.

"Well, if the church gives consent then the sign can be posted as long as it is one hundred feet away from the building," she said. Again.

The poll worker quietly gave me my license back and directed me to another worker who gave me a ballot and directions to enter it to be counted. I did so. As I exited I could feel their eyes on me as I walked away with my 'I Voted' sticker.

I stopped and asked the church security guard the same question to which I got a swift and puzzled 'I don't know' as I walked away. The poll worker who greeted me as I entered spoke to me as I was leaving. She said that a campaign volunteer asked to put the signs there early that morning and had tried to put them next to the door but had to move them to the regulation one hundred feet distance. I told her that I didn't care about who the sign was for but rather the fact that the sign was there. She said that she understood and for me to have a good day. I returned the sentiment as I exited the double doors and walked to my SUV.

Unsatisfied I sat in the driver's seat and called the Supervisor of Elections Office. I would get a straight answer today if I had to petition the U.S. Supreme Court. A few rings, an automated answer, and two transfers later I spoke to a person who might have been able to answer my questions. I reiterated my concern and she answered saying the same rote one hundred feet rule to which I asked about exceptions for churches. She said that churches are private property and if signs are posted they must be posted with permission of the property holder. She took my name and number saying that she would call back with a more comprehensive answer.

I never got a call back.

After hanging up I sent a quick message to a friend of mine who was an attorney to get her take on it.

I wrote:

Good morning. Happy Primary! I just called the Supervisor

of Elections and made a complaint about campaign signs on actual church property. Am I correct in the fact that due to separation of church and state campaign materials cannot be posted on actual church property? There are signs in the parking lot, which constitutes private church property, and even though they are 100 ft. from the bldg the bldg itself is a church. Just my two cents...

Two minutes later she wrote:

I totally agree with you, first and foremost. I don't know how they get around having elections in churches and what not. I have a good friend who works for the supervisor of elections I'm asking that question. I'll tag you in it if you like and you can follow his response. He also happens to be a constitutional lawyer so I think he'll have a good interesting take on it. Happy election day!

I put the phone back on the charger and reached for the gear shift. In my side view I saw the poll worker that greeted me walk into the parking lot and over to the sign. She picked it up and laid it on the ground. I smiled to myself. Civic duty for the day, done. I picked up my phone and wrote:

Sure. I talked to the site supervisor...no clue. I called the Supervisor of Elections...didn't know. Someone had posted signs at my church Sunday and the pastor sent security to take them down. How do the poll workers NOT understand basic constitutional law? I waited in the lot for a while and a poll worker took them down. I think that they should stop using churches as voting precincts. IMHO

I won't get into the fact that I don't think that churches should be used as polling places. What I will offer is that the ground they are built on should be consecrated holy and the main sanctuary is a place of worship and not a recreation center to entertain. Our souls go there to be fed and not pandered to. Our population is not some faction to be courted on Sunday morning with a carefully selected scripture vetted by a campaign manager. My vote is not for sale especially in the name of the Lord. That's just my two cents...

I am the primary caregiver to a child with special needs. I listen to the candidates degrade each other. I watch the candidates' actions toward each other. I watch the candidates exploit each other's differences. They throw rocks and hide their hands. They craft words to puff themselves up even at the expense of someone else who they campaign to govern. I hear them in the morning. I see them at noon. I see them at night. I see them but they do not see me.

I belong to a specific subset of the population rarely seen on the campaign trail. They don't see the hurt these words cause daily in our lives. They don't see the fight that we undertake just to be included in the activities most people take for granted. They can't possibly understand the effect that the programs they cut have on families that depend on them to give our disabled loved ones a decent quality of life. They talk about education but cannot fathom the struggle we have in getting an IEP (individualized education program) written effectively to give our children the support they need. And they taught, 'No Child Left Behind'. They bicker over submitting tax returns and how much someone was paid to speak at a convention. I wish that they could see my tax returns or any other mom who had to give up her career to take care of a child with special needs. Our children aren't left behind for sure. They just aren't readily seen.

You may not see us but we are here. We are not lazy by any means. We are strong beyond measure. We are advocates and caregivers and tired and frustrated and courageous and invisible. We are not on any stage behind a podium. We are not included in any campaign slogan. We are not in any meme circulated on social media. We are not a superset of any platform. We are neither a Super Pac nor primary monetary contributors. It's Super Tuesday and I haven't heard one super word that would help our population. I watch the commercials. I search the internet. I have found nothing that will make me favor any candidate over another as it concerns my family. Nada. Zip. Zilch. Zero. Yet in some respect everything they say affects my family in some way.

If I could have I would have voted 'KINDNESS' for President. It wasn't on the ballot. Perhaps it should have been. I wonder if it would get the nomination uncontested. We'll never know.

I pulled out of the parking space and drove toward the front entrance. I heard "DING DING DING" again as I drove past the downed sign. I smiled. I'm a Mighty Mom. I'm a Super Mom. It's Super Tuesday and if you look real hard you'll see my cape blow in the wind.

And you'll see it if I have to push this SUV to the gas station. Literally.

Inclusion is for the Included

Inclusion is for the Included

BONUS

FIFTY DIMES AND A WRAPPER

"Your mama birthed you, but you MY baby."
~Mattie Henry

My grandmother kept a small tin can in the top of her chifferobe. What is a chifferobe, you ask? It's what many commonly refer to as an armoire, a piece of furniture with both drawers and hanging space for keeping clothing. A chifferobe, however, also had a mirrored front to either one or both doors. Her room did not have a closet and the chifferobe was the solution. Often she would give me loose change to put in the can.

"Why do you put change in this can, Mama?" I would ask.

"That's for a rainy day, Baby...." she would reply.

In my young mind I had no idea what money and rain had to do with each other, but I was happy that she entrusted me with this task. So off I would go to retrieve the tin and bring it to her.

"Now take the lid off and pour out the change on this table." she instructed. "Spread it out flat."

So I did that. Spread it out flat.

"Now we're gonna separate the quarters, nickels, dimes and pennies. Put them in little piles."

So I did that. Put them in little piles.

"Now I need you to count fifty dimes." she said.

"I can't count to fifty, Mama." I replied.

"Yes you can. You can count to ten can't you?" she said with that 'matter of fact' look she would always have.

"Yes ma'am." I replied, just as puzzled as ever.

"Well you can count to fifty. Let's count to ten FIVE TIMES."

So I picked up my dimes one at a time and stacked them into little piles of ten. Occasionally, I would put the stacks a little too close together and they would fall into one mass conglomerate.

"Do it again." she said.

So I did that. I did it again.

Before long I not only had the dimes stacked, but, per instruction, stacks of ten pennies, ten nickels, and four quarters. Next came the part that puzzled me even more.

"Now put five of these stacks of dimes in this wrapper. Lemme show you...put your finger in the bottom and hold it in your hand. Now pick up one stack and put it in this wrapper. Don't take your finger out. Tap it in there and then you'll have a dollar."

WHAAAAAAA??????? A DOLLAR???? NOBODY SAID ANYTHING ABOUT A DOLLAR!!!

Now you know that this had to be a long time ago because I was HA-A-APPY to get a dollar. Children these days ask for at least $5. Sometimes $20. Mama said do it this way and after a few attempts my little hands held fifty dimes in a paper wrapper.

"Now what do I do, Mama?" I asked.

"Give it to me. Watch how I fold the end." My little eyes could not figure out how those little corners folded so neat. My grandmother had large hands for a woman who only stood 5'2" on her tip toes. But she had a heart that was 10-feet-tall. "Now you tap it down like this and that makes it stay. Your money won't fall out."

She opened the ends back up and gave the dimes to me. I did what I saw her doing and I tapped the dimes on the table....and they all came falling out.

"Do it again." she said.

So I did that. I did it again.

Before long I could count out all the coins, pick the correct wrapper, wrap them up, fold the corners, tap the table and count the stacks.

"How much do we have today, Baby?" she would ask.

"About $20, Mama." I answered.

"Put it with rest then. Take out a roll of dimes."

"Where do I put the dimes, Mama?"

"You keep them. That's for a rainy day."

ACKNOWLEDGMENTS

I am most thankful to God, the Father, the Creator, the Author and Finisher of my faith. Enough said.

As for the earthly vessels, I thank my mother, Gloria Waddell, for always being the wind in my sails and the one constant in a world of uncertainties. She has always been my biggest cheerleader and champion for my numerous endeavors. I am forever grateful for the values that she has given me and the 'lead by example' attitude she has exemplified in raising a daughter who is now raising a daughter. Thank you for not only being you, but just BEING. I love you.

Thanks to my daughter, Cairo, for being the inspiration for the stories that I write. You are my heartbeat and though you throw me into cardiac arrest most days I love you with everything that I have. I cannot imagine a life without you. I will fight for you until my last breath and then watch over you from above. You saved my life. And I am in your debt for it. I love you, too.

Thanks to all the friends, family, and clients alike who lent an ear to listen and a shoulder to cry on. It truly takes a village to raise a child and I thank you for being residents. A special thank you goes to my dear friend Jackie Brockington for being my Day One on this journey. It is rare to find someone who 'gets' you and I am proud to say that you, my dear, are a true FRIEND. I love you, too.

Another special thanks goes to Tricia Higgins and Abbey Dryden from the Pampers Division at Proctor and Gamble for recognizing the first piece I ever wrote about my daughter. The campaign, Every Little Miracle, touched me in a special way and I am grateful for the kindness and compassion it took to bring inclusion to the forefront and show that children with special needs are miracles too. Though it was only a simple letter it was truly heartfelt and I appreciate the friendship we continue to share. You both are honorary Aunties.

To my family and those who have become my extended family here in Orlando: all the doctors, therapists, specialists, the Down Syndrome Association of Central Florida, the Down Syndrome Foundation of Central Florida, and the Macedonia Missionary Baptist Church family: thanks to you all.

I'd like to recognize those who helped bring this project to fruition. Thank you to the most wonderful photographer in the whole wide world, the incomparable Angelo Davis of A Davis Photography for always coming through in a clutch for me and my family. Thank you to Tanika Ault of Legacy Designs by Tanika c/o Graceful Lion Creations LLC for listening to my rambling descriptions and turning them into fantastic logos and cover art. Thank you to Nekisha L. Killings and The Grace of God, Inc. for keeping me on schedule and bringing my words to the masses. Thanks also to Maurice Robinson of Robinson and Robinson, Inc. for handling the accounting aspects of this project.

But perhaps most of all, to my beloved Mattie, whose decimation of the English language made growing up that much sweeter. Rest easy my sweet. Rest easy.

Inclusion is for the Included

ABOUT THE AUTHOR

La Taasha Byrd is a stay-at-home-mom to one daughter born with Down Syndrome. She holds a Bachelor of Science degree in Biology from Florida Agricultural and Mechanical University and a Master of Science degree in Criminal Justice from the University of Central Florida. She hails from the metropolis of Monticello, Florida where she learned the values of small town life and a love for country living. She is a proud, self-proclaimed 'Mom-Schooler' and chronicles the journey of homeschooling a child with exceptionality in her Facebook blog, Countdown To K. Together she and her daughter reside in Orlando, FL where they enjoy many activities in the Florida sun.

Inclusion is for the Included

www.ingramcontent.com/pod-product-compliance
Lightning Source LLC
LaVergne TN
LVHW041544070426
835507LV00011B/921